MARX AND AMERICA

MARX AND AMERICA

A Study of the Doctrine of Impoverishment

By EARL BROWDER

DUELL, SLOAN AND PEARCE

New York

Library of Congress Catalogue Card Number: 58-12263

First edition

MANUFACTURED IN THE UNITED STATES OF AMERICA

VAN REES PRESS • NEW YORK

To the memory of Raissa

who understood and loved America

AUTHOR'S NOTE

THIS BOOK grew out of lectures delivered at Rutgers University, New Brunswick, New Jersey, in November 1957, and expanded in a series of lectures at the New School For Social Research, New York City, in the summer session, 1958.

All references to *Capital* deal with Volume I of the Kerr edition; those to *Karl Marx: Selected Works,* Volumes 1 and 2, deal with the International Publishers edition printed in the U.S.S.R., and containing most of the best-known pamphlets of Marx and Engels; *Anti-Dühring,* or *Herr Eugen Dühring's Revolution in Science* by Frederick Engels, refers to the edition of International Publishers of 1939; *Selected Correspondence* refers to the International Publishers edition of 1942 under the full title *The Selected Correspondence of Karl Marx and Frederick Engels, 1846–1895; Imperialism and World Economy,* by Nikolai Bukharin, refers to the International Publishers edition of 1929; *The Civil War in the United States* by Marx and Engels is the 1937 edition of International Publishers. Other references are identified in the text or footnotes.

CONTENTS

INTRODUCTION

AMERICA has nothing to worry about so far as Marx's theory is concerned. The feature of it pointing particularly to revolution was the contention that capitalism inevitably deprives the mass of the workers until their misery becomes intolerable. Marx himself made an exception of America, though he thought the higher wages prevailing here as compared with Europe would not continue indefinitely to exempt this country from his gloomy forecast. Also at one period he embraced in his doctrine the concession that wages need not sink to the level of mere physical subsistence, but might include enough to permit the workers a standard of living to which they had become firmly habituated. This admission undoes the prediction that the proletarians will be driven to desperate remedies.

However, immunity of America from revolutionary fate is only partial reassurance. Marx has given morals to half the world. It does not matter that his economic dicta are dimly guessed by millions who acknowledge him. Among depressed peoples much supplies the place of precise textual agreement. National resurgence, racial claims, envy of the more advanced countries, native pride that challenges misfortune—all of these eagerly proclaim that Marx, with excellent cause, has won emotional loyalty against which rational remonstrance makes uncertain headway. Our own security will be tenuous until, combining works with faith, we exert ourselves mightily to cancel the centuries of western heedlessness and presumption.

Marx's imperfect understanding of America sprang from several causes. He was never here and could not fully estimate the resources of this continent and the expansion of which our economy was capable. What was before his eyes was the plight of workers in Europe, worse cramped by the progress of industrialism. Equally important, he accepted the philosophy of writers who preceded him, and pressed their foreboding to the logical conclusion. His dogma reflected his time and place, and was not applicable in different circumstances.

Mr. Browder, from long study and exceptional opportunity of acquaintance with the world Marxist movement, puts this point with engaging clarity. He discourages the notion of Marx and Engels as universal prophets. Rather, they were original thinkers and courageous advocates needing to be appraised in their peculiar setting. Not fully perceived by them, America was giving capitalism a second wind. With enormous productivity, political talents, and technological ingenuity, this country could avoid disasters that impended elsewhere. American economists were saying as much, but unhappily Marx and Engels disparaged their optimism. Ironically, these European analysts, who did more than others to impress the lesson of history, did not guess the turn that history in the new world would take. And, as Mr. Browder aptly shows, energies from America, moral and material, are invigorating tired social tissues in many alien lands.

This progress, if nuclear war does not first explode mankind, can resolve excited antagonisms that now plague us. Given time, nations and peoples may improve in plenty and justice and peace. A formula of fateful misery, nobly honest in inception but fallacious in experience, has become the common enemy.

Hearing Mr. Browder's lectures, I was quick to beg that he publish them, not only for his welcome analysis of Marx's conception of America, but as an injunction to America to form a just conception of Marx. He has kindly acted on the proposal, expanding his chapters to include a revealing appraisal of world tensions.

BROADUS MITCHELL

New Brunswick
New Jersey

MARX AND AMERICA

I.

MARX'S AMBIGUITY REGARDING AMERICA

KARL MARX was a man of positive and sharply defined opinions. With regard to America, however, he displayed an ambiguity that was never overcome. He saw America in two quite different images, both of them clear but contradictory to each other. One was that of an America leading the world in political and economic progress; the other he described as an "undeveloped" land that was, "speaking economically, still only a colony of Europe." The Marxist school of thought never escaped from this ambiguity of its founder.

The contradiction here was not of the type that Marx delighted to find in the *raw material* with which he worked, the unraveling of which was his chief method to reach beneath the surface to grasp the essence of problems. This was a contradiction within Marx's own mind, of which he hardly seemed conscious, and which he certainly never resolved. His two images of America were shown on different planes of thought and never brought into direct juxtaposition. Whenever he looked at America either in the broad panorama of past history or in the immediacy of concrete economic and political problems, he was unstinting in his recognition of America's dynamic qualities. But when he looked at America from the viewpoint of the norms of capitalist economy as he had elaborated these norms in his theoretical system, he invariably judged America as backward and undeveloped, doomed to follow the lead and pattern of the "more developed capitalism," that is, England. It did not enter Marx's mind to ask whether the norms of capitalist development might be more correctly set by America, and therefore be different from those drawn from English experience. Since England was the older, richer, and larger economy with established predominance in the world market, this issue was decided for Marx by his assumption that

> "The country that is more developed industrially only shows, to the less developed, the image of its own future." (*Capital,* p. 13.)

Marx made his monumental study of capitalism in the middle years of the nineteenth century. He built upon the foundations laid by classical English political economy. England was the foremost industrial country, the world's workshop and banker. It was inevitable that Marx should take England as his norm, furthermore, because concerning England there was the most voluminous collection of facts and the richest literature discussing them, all of which Marx found at his command in the British Museum. He was fully conditioned to set his norms on the English model, and there is no sign that he ever questioned the universal validity of those norms. Thus when he found that America stood outside of that pattern, he did not ask if the pattern should be changed to make room for America, but only how America must change to conform to the pattern.

This is the root of Marx's ambiguity regarding America, and, given the dogmatic tendency of his disciples, the root of later Marxism's feebleness on all questions that were decisively influenced by America.

America stood outside the Marxist norm of capitalism most notably in her high wages and living standards, which contradicted the doctrine of impoverishment as the "absolute general law of capitalist accumulation." It has been a grave shortcoming in economic thought, however, to rest content with this practical refutation of the doctrine of impoverishment, without pursuing the question into the depths of economic theory. For as long as the doctrine is not refuted in detail, it will keep coming back to haunt America in new forms. And so long as the great majority of the world's population lives in poverty, so long also will the theory of impoverishment as the "absolute law of capitalist accumulation" remain potent among them. In the material prosperity of America they will see its *proof* rather than its *refutation,* with America's wealth as the opposite pole to their own misery, in a mutual relationship of cause-and-effect. Most of the world lives today with this thought, which is the chief ingredient of anti-Americanism. The Communists make much use of it, but they didn't invent or create the idea—it is much deeper than propaganda. In the interests of a peaceful understanding among nations, if for no other reason, it has become important to gain a deeper understanding of this whole question.

Every rich uncle has traditionally felt that all his poor nephews and nieces should feel respect, gratitude, and love for him, and Uncle Sam is no exception. And he, like all the others, feels outraged when he finds most of his relatives see him rather as Uncle Shylock the miser, whose riches are coined from the blood and flesh of others. The American response to this, far from tending to remedy the situation, usually makes it worse.

Now it so happened that Marx and his co-worker Engels, whose formulation of the doctrine of impoverishment is today its most influential variation, were not among those who explained the material prosperity of America by its supposed robbery of other nations. Quite the contrary, and those modern Communists who do so in the name of Marx are illiterates or mendacious.[1]

Marx and Engels made some serious theoretical mistakes about America, but they never engaged in such stupidities as this. In fact they showed in much detail how American living standards rose above the rest of the world because of the relatively free relations of American producers, the existence of free land, and the more democratic society and institutions that grew up on that basis. And theoretically they proved that nations cannot be enriched by robbing others, that in the rise of capitalism, as Engels put it, "The whole process is explained by purely economic causes; robbery, force, the state or political interference of any kind are unnecessary at any point whatever. 'Property founded on force' proves here also to be nothing but the phrase of a braggart intended to cover up his lack of understanding of the real course of things." (*Anti-Dühring,* p. 181.) And Marx exclaimed: "How disastrous it is for a nation when it has subjugated another nation." One does not explain the rise of a world power by its disasters.

America refuted in practice the dogma of impoverishment as the necessary accompaniment of accumulation, without being conscious of how it was done, and without mastering

[1] For example, the thesis that the United States "during all the time of their existence" followed "an exploiters and robbers policy" and grew rich and strong by "drinking greedily the rich red blood" of other nations, is developed in 668 pages of *Outline Political History of the Americas* by Wm. Z. Foster. This illiterate parody on Marxism was read by hardly anyone in America, but was extravagantly praised by Moscow publications, and translated into many languages all over the world.

any later explanation of its secret. Re-examining the thought of Marx on America we will gain many brilliant insights into this problem, for with Marx there is profit even in studying his mistakes, and these were not so many. We find all the elements of Marx's ambiguity about America, as well as his deep insight, in Chapter XXXIII of *Capital,* the only section of his work that is mainly concerned with America. Disputing with some reactionary English economists, chiefly E. G. Wakefield, who wrote books advocating that Canada, Australia, and New Zealand should have imposed upon them by legislation the same capital-labor relationships that existed in England in order that British capital might feel secure in investing there, Marx notes that he deals with the United States in the same frame of reference. He explains this by saying: "The United States are, speaking economically, still only a colony of Europe." Then he continues:

> In the colonies [in which he includes the U.S.A.] the capitalist regime comes everywhere into collision with the resistance of the producer, who, as owner of his own conditions of labor, employs that labor to enrich himself, instead of the capitalist. The contradiction of these two diametrically opposed economic systems manifests itself practically in a struggle between them. (*Capital,* p. 838.)

Here Marx has made the most emphatic possible distinction between England and America; he speaks of them as two diametrically opposed economic systems.[2]

Marx is not denying here that America had a modern industry similar to that of the British. Indeed, some fifteen

[2] It is of interest to note that exactly this phrase was chosen to describe the Soviet-American contradiction in the Moscow declaration of the Conference of Communist Parties held November 14–16, 1957. Here is an intimation, perhaps unconscious, that this current contradiction is no more permanent than the British-American contradiction described by Marx in 1867.

years earlier he had written, in *The Eighteenth Brumaire,* a description of America where he says:

> ... The United States of North America where, though classes, indeed, already exist, they have not yet become fixed, but change and interchange their elements in a constant state of flux, where the modern means of production, instead of coinciding with a stagnant surplus population, rather supply the relative deficiency of heads and hands, and where, finally, the feverishly youthful movement of material production ... has a new world to make its own. ... (Marx, *Selected Works,* Vol. 2, pp. 324–5.)

Here Marx emphasizes the *absence* in America of that stagnant surplus population which he considered the necessary "basis" of the capitalist mode of production, and the *presence* of the modern means of production. This is the essential element that made it possible for him to speak of England and America as "two diametrically opposed economic systems." In England the bulk of the people were driven from the land, and those who remained as cultivators were mainly tenants and wage workers, thus creating a stagnant surplus population upon which rose the capitalist mode of production. In America there arose a modern apparatus of production on the basis of a relative scarcity of heads and hands. In England Marx says the stagnant surplus population was essential in the "absolute general law of capitalist accumulation." In America Marx notes the rise of modern means of production, the concrete form of accumulation, without the presence of a stagnant surplus population.

Marx certainly was in no doubt that the American economy was capitalist in nature, even though "diametrically opposed" to the British. Even the then predominant sector of the economy represented by individual producers working on their own account, the farmers, artisans, individual tradesmen, was engaged in commodity production and distribution for the world market more completely than any other country. Engels, as early as 1844, was registering the rapid advance of America in competition with the British on the capitalist world market, and predicting American supremacy in the foreseeable future. In *Conditions of the Working Class in England,* Engels observed:

> America, with its inexhaustible resources, with its unmeasured coal and iron fields, with its unexampled wealth of water-power and its navigable rivers, *but especially with its energetic, active population,* in comparison with which the English are phlegmatic dawdlers—America has in less than ten years created a manufacture which already competes with England in the coarser cotton goods, has excluded the English from the markets of North and South America, and holds its own in China side by side with England. If any country is adapted to holding a monopoly of manufacture, it is America.

There is little point in multiplying quotations from Marx and Engels, showing how they recognized that in America their "absolute law" of impoverishment was not applicable, but that nevertheless in America accumulation of capital was proceeding more rapidly than in England. This recognition of American experience that contradicted the "absolute law" runs throughout their writings from 1844 onward. We will quote further only as we penetrate deeper into the theory of the matter.

It will lay a solid basis for a deeper examination of Marx's theoretical system and the ambiguous position of America in it, if we reconstruct the picture of American development *as Marx saw it,* for the period from the Revolution to 1867 when the first volume of *Capital* was published. The following condensed summary does not go beyond the boundaries of Marx's own recorded observations.

When the thirteen British colonies liberated themselves in

the Revolutionary War of Independence and established the United States of America, this country already possessed an economy which, in its basic structure, was more advanced than that of Western Europe and in some ways even of England. Its agriculture was, more than any European land, predominantly one of commodity production for the world market. Its iron production and fabrication, and general manufactures, compared favorably with those of England. The Revolution wiped out the semi-feudal colonial governments, and with them the social-economic remnants of feudalism, such as titles of nobility, quitrents, entails, primogeniture, tithes, and clerical domination in government. The great landed estates were broken up and, together with immense public lands, were distributed as small farms. Even chattel slavery, which remained in the South as the unfinished business of the Revolution until the Civil War of 1861–65, was wiped out in the North by legal action by 1800. Slavery was expected to die a quiet death because of its growing unprofitability but, by an irony of history, the invention of the cotton gin, a great technological advance, injected new profits into the dying institution and thereby caused the Civil War.

In short, the distinctive achievement of America was the abolition of almost all the remnants of pre-capitalist political and economic institutions and practices. The one conspicuous exception was slavery until the Civil War, and its remnants which only after another century are now being cleaned up in the sharpest struggles of domestic politics. Despite this one important exception to the rule, the United States is the unique example of a great nation which, from its foundation, proceeded to sweep away antiquated institutions and folkways incompatible with the needs of modern society. Thus America has the "purest" capitalism, that is, it has the smallest intermixture of precapitalist remnants. This sweeping character of the American Revolution was the chief factor in bestowing upon this country, in final outcome, the position of world economic supremacy, by wiping out those hindrances to economic progress from the past, which in Europe and England persisted into the late nineteenth century and even to the present day.

The central factor in America's exceptionally favorable situation as compared with England and Europe lay in the system of free land in contrast with the closed-land monopoly of the Old World. Marx perceived this more clearly than any other economist of his time, and analyzed it more deeply. That he failed to perceive *all* the consequences in the shaping of capitalist economy simply means that Marx was not, as some fanatical followers imply, a superman or god from another world, but simply the greatest thinker of his time, a head taller than his contemporaries but essentially one of them. Marx could not see that the American free land system furnished a refutation to the dogmas of impoverishment and the subsistence wage, not simply as a temporary obstacle, but more fundamentally as opening the way for the emergence of contrary forces that gave another direction to world development.

Thus arose the contradiction within Marx's thought about America, its ambiguous character that points in two directions simultaneously. Marx was far too intelligent to fail to see, and too rigorously honest to fail to register, all the facts in the America of his time that went contrary to his dogma of impoverishment as the absolute law of capitalist accumulation. But he was too much the prisoner of this dogma to relinquish it. He saved the dogma, however, not by denying the facts as do his modern dogmatic disciples, but by judging these facts to be temporary hindrances to the operation of the underlying economic laws, as signs of the "undeveloped" character of America in the capitalist sense, and as doomed to be obliterated in the further development of American capitalism along the predetermined pattern earlier displayed by England's rise.

Let us sum up this first bird's-eye survey of the contradictory position of America in the Marxist system of thought.

On the one hand, Marx, judging America by norms and theories drawn from the study of England and from the established classical British political economy, and assuming that capitalist development in other lands must follow the same pattern, says that America is "undeveloped" and as yet without the necessary conditions for the accumulation of capital on the scale required by the existing stage of technology and, therefore, "speaking economically, still only a colony of Europe." This is Marx the dogmatist.

On the other hand Marx, accepting facts as sacred and precious in their own right, freely and fully registers those facts which contradict his dogmas, namely: that the American economy was already superior to the English in his time, and would soon surpass it in every way; that nevertheless the American people were not being impoverished, but that they were well-to-do, independent, enterprising, and comparatively cultured; that American production, under a wage level two and more times that of England, was successfully competing with products in the world market and even in England itself. This is Marx the scientific analyst.

If in the final outcome the dogmas are to be overthrown in the minds of men, this will be done most expeditiously and completely if we enlist the help of Marx the scientific analyst.

A century of struggles and controversies has raised high obstacles to the understanding of Marx's thought. Perhaps the greatest of these has been the agreement, between enemies and adherents of Marx, that his thought is an organic whole that must be either accepted or rejected in its entirety. If that were true, it would be the first such case in the history of the human mind. But of course it is not true, and as a matter of fact, in real life nobody, literally nobody, actually follows such a course. Those who protest most loudly that they reject Marx *in toto* have, even if they do not know it, silently adopted into their thought and views of the world a great part of Marx's contribution to the general body of thought, because Marx changed the intellectual climate of the whole human race. And the dogmatic Marxists, who abstractly oppose the change of even a comma in Marx's writings, are in fact by their "interpretations" among the most drastic revisionists of Marxism. Everyone is a revisionist even if he disagrees upon what is to be revised. In our modern world with its capitalism that Marx would not have been able to recognize if he had seen it—even as he would find great difficulty in recognizing our current "socialism"—no one finds it really possible to accept or reject Marxism "as a whole," no matter how loudly he protests that he does so.

It has become historically expedient, however, even if we are hesitant to use the strong word "necessary," to make a more serious effort to understand Marx, forgetting about the false issue as to whether he is to be "accepted" or "rejected" as though one were dealing with a religious system. For everyone the serious question is a detailed separation of the wheat from the chaff, the science from the dogma.

Those who prefer to deal with chaff and dogma, whether to extol or denounce, may cling to that side of Marx as is their right in any free society. Those who prefer wheat and science will gain much profit from such critical study, even though the intellectual labor involved may be painful. Very few, in the modern world, can be satisfied with the "all or nothing" attitude toward Marx.

Many efforts were made in the course of the past century, among adherents of Marxism, to break out of the bonds of dogmatism at those points most sharply in conflict with reality, the dogmas of impoverishment and the subsistence wage. The most widely known of these efforts was initiated in the German Social-Democratic party by Eduard Bernstein at the close of the nineteenth century, and was defeated by the "orthodox" section of the party led by Karl Kautsky, one of the most authoritative original disciples of Marx. That whole discussion, and similar ones at other times and places, has only a peripheral significance for our present study, however, because it appeared as a revolt of "practical men" against the "tyranny of theory." And while it is true that all human thought, even the most abstract, must look for its final validation by reference to the real world existing outside the realm of thought and furnishing its raw material, yet this real world of practicality very rarely overthrows an established theory unless and until it is given a superior theory, or a more realistic version of the old theory. In the realm of thought, theory will always triumph over the absence of theory, whatever may be the defects it harbors. We can therefore find no light for the present from the old Bernstein-Kautsky controversy.

The great dogmatic revisionists, Lenin and Stalin, on the other hand, made the most drastic revisions of Marx but always in the name of, and not as opposed to, theory. Indeed, they always claimed to be the most orthodox of all, and to the degree that orthodoxy is synonymous with dogmatism they were justified in that claim. They brought Marxism closer to the underdeveloped countries which had firsthand experience with capitalism only in its most primitive forms, and as a revolutionary impact from outside shattering their pre-capitalist economies. But they widened the gap between the Marxist dogmas and the countries of the industrialized West, where capitalism had developed beyond the framework of those dogmas. Thus the second great school of revisionism, like the first, has only peripheral significance for our present restudy of Marx. Not only can we take neither as even an approximate model, but we find in them only an occasional flash of insight into the problems we are here facing.

If Marx's key mistakes regarding America's coming role loom ever larger in our study, I would suggest to the reader never to forget that Marx was, with all his inner contradictions and all such mistakes, the most inspiring and germinal mind of the modern era, the most pervasive single influence in the creation of the intellectual standards and climate of our day. It is irrational if we should underrate him, because he did not solve all modern problems, or for failing in one or another matter, even as it would be irrational to underrate Isaac Newton because he did not give us the concepts of relativity that had to wait for Einstein.

There is much in common in the historical roles of Isaac Newton and Karl Marx. This realization came to me recently as I was reading Andrade's brilliant essay on the tercentenary of Newton (*The World of Mathematics,* Simon & Schuster, New York, 1956, Vol. I, pp. 255–76). Here I found my own attitude to Marx expressed with an accuracy for which I had not myself found words. Before proceeding further to assault a few of Marx's dogmas, I take the liberty of borrowing a few words from Andrade, leaves from the laurels of the scientist Newton to lay before the scientist Marx:

From time to time in the history of mankind a man arises who is of universal significance, whose work changes the current of human thought, so that all that comes after bears evidence of his spirit. The face of science changes, theories fail and rise again transformed. Achievement such as Marx's is not lessened by the advances of subsequent centuries; it survives in undiminished strength and beauty. Marx's thought has grown to be a universal study, a shining example of the exalted power of the human mind.

II.

AMERICA'S EXCEPTIONAL POSITION

MARX clearly recognized America's exceptional position, demonstrated by its deviation from his doctrine of impoverishment or "pauperism" as the "absolute general law of capitalist accumulation." This exceptional position must have had exceptional causes. It is now our task to locate and define them.

Marx did not invent or discover the doctrine of impoverishment. He found it ready made in the political economy of his time, and merely took it over, analyzed it, rationalized and refined it, and turned it into a revolutionary criticism of the existing social order. He found, for example, in the writings of DeStutt de Tracy, a prominent French economist, a condensation of that doctrine into an axiom that he preserved for posterity. De Tracy had written:

"In poor nations the people are comfortable; in rich nations they are generally poor." (Cited by Marx, *Capital,* p. 711.)

The intuition was general that the rise of modern industrial production inevitably brought with it the polarization of the nation into the rich and richer on top, and the poor and ever poorer at the bottom. It permeated the popular consciousness as well as the reasoned analyses of political economy. It was the burden of all the various utopian socialist appeals. A typical voice of this popular feeling was the poet who sang:

> Ill fares the land, to hastening ills a prey,
> Where wealth accumulates and men decay.
>
> (Oliver Goldsmith)

Marx focused this almost universal presentiment into the form of a scientific law founded on the analysis of hard facts.

David Ricardo, of the generation before Marx, was a successful stock-market operator before he became a noted economist. His theoretical writings provided Marx with his first foundations in serious economic study, and Marx always expressed a high opinion of him. In his early works he was one of the few economists who insisted that the laboring classes gained some benefits from the development of machinery, but in the third edition of his *Principles of Political Economy and Taxation,* published in 1821, he reversed himself and said: "The substitution of machinery for human labor is often very injurious to the interests of the class of laborers." He explained his change with the observation that "The same cause which may increase the net revenue of the country may at the same time render the population redundant, and deteriorate the condition of the laborer." Marx praised Ricardo for this right-about-face, as a sign of his honesty and integrity. Nor was Ricardo alone in this view. Marx's contemporary, John Stuart Mill, perhaps the last of the great classical school, wrote in 1848: "It is questionable if all the mechanical inventions yet made have lightened the day's toil of any human being."

Thus Marx, in accepting the doctrine of impoverishment as a necessary result of capitalist accumulation, was in harmony with the main body of economic thought which he inherited. Where Marx sharply departed from the established view was in making use of the doctrine to prove the necessity of a revolutionary transformation of the economic system. Even on this point of criticism of capitalism as a system, Marx was not alone, although no other economist of note went nearly so far as he. An outstanding example was J. S. Mill, who wrote of capitalism as a transitional system, and said:

> ... If the institution of private property necessarily carried with it as a consequence, that the produce of labor should be apportioned as we now see it, almost in inverse ratio to the labor ... if this or communism were the alternative, all the difficulties, great or small, of communism would be but as dust in the balance.

As Marx refined this established doctrine of impoverishment, the necessary base for the rise of capitalism was the existence of a surplus or redundant population which, divorced from the land, had no other means of livelihood than employment as wage labor. This surplus population grows ever greater in relation to available employment, not only because of the pressure of population growth (stressed by Malthus and Ricardo), but more especially because capitalist relations and the growth of productivity serve to reproduce the original surplus population on an expanding scale. Marx called this surplus population the "industrial reserve army," and its presence he saw as providing an absolute limit to the operation of supply and demand as a factor favoring the worker, serving on the contrary to "complete the despotism of capital." Therefore the inherent urge of the employer to purchase labor power as cheaply as possible meets no check short of the subsistence necessary to keep the laborer at work and provide his replacement. Even this limitation may be transgressed when demand for labor slackens for any reason, and the actual worker may undergo pauperization on the job, living below the subsistence level for a time. All the more, therefore, does pauperization ravage the industrial reserve army which, partially or totally unemployed, sinks more or less rapidly into degradation and official pauperism on a scale that increases with the increased accumulation of capital as its "absolute general law." This doctrine of impoverishment is given a further theoretical buttress by the theory that the value of labor power is determined by subsistence, that quantity of commodities necessary to maintain the worker and below which poverty begins, and that this value in the long run determines the general level of wages.

America was for more than a century and a half a demonstration that the "general law" was not "absolute" in the sense of applying rigorously and at all times to capitalist accumulation. Around the turn of the eighteenth and nineteenth centuries the American wage level was approximately twice as high as that of England, corresponding to the generally higher standard of life in the country as a whole. This gap in favor of America widened with the passing of years. Therefore, even if it should be accepted that the "absolute law" was valid for England, it was clearly not operative for America. Marx himself was among the first to record this fact, and document it in great detail. He saved the theory by explaining it was the result of the "undeveloped" status of the American economy.

In the United States of America (and to a lesser degree in Canada, Australia, and New Zealand) Marx explained that the law of supply and demand fell to pieces as the instrument to "complete the despotism of capital" as in England. The population increased here even more than elsewhere, yet the labor market was always understocked. The wage worker of today was tomorrow an independent farmer, or an artisan working on his own account, vanishing from the labor market but not into the poorhouse. Those who consented to be wage workers were able to secure so considerable a share in the product of their labor that they soon became capitalists themselves on the restricted scale then general. Very few men were in a position to amass big personal fortunes, but the mass of the population was well-to-do, independent, enterprising, and comparatively cultured—these descriptions are drawn from *Capital,* and are either Marx's own or are quoted by him as accurate. It is a picture of America in the first half of the nineteenth century, and in comparison with the regime described in the law of impoverishment, the two appear indeed as "two diametrically opposed economic systems" as Marx described them.

Remembering always that when Marx is speaking of a "free colony" he is including the United States of America in that category, the following quotation will give us an essential feature of Marx's thought concerning America. He writes:

> We have seen that the expropriation of the mass of the people from the soil forms the basis of the capitalist mode of production. The essence of the free colony, on the contrary, consists in this—the bulk of the soil is still public property, and every settler on it therefore can turn part of it into his private property and individual means of production, without hindering the later settlers in the same operation. This is the secret both of the prosperity of the colonies and their inveterate vice—opposition to the establishment of capital. (Marx, *Capital,* pp. 841–2.)

If we now recall Marx's observation, previously quoted, that America possessed the modern means of production without a surplus population, and with a wage scale twice as high as England's, it becomes apparent that *under the laws of capitalist accumulation and of wages* either as formulated by Marx or Ricardo (or indeed by any other of the classical economists) *it is impossible to explain the rise of modern industry in America.* I refer specifically to their common assumption that "the expropriation of the people from the soil forms the basis of the capitalist mode of production," and the three consequent "laws": (a) the law of pauperism as the condition and result of capitalist accumulation, (b) the law that though real wages may rise, they cannot rise in proportion to the rise in productivity, and (c) the law that the value of labor power, final determinant of wages, is to be resolved into a definite quantity of commodities representing bare subsistence.

If this assumption and the three laws, common to Ricardo and Marx with only the difference that the latter analyzed them much more completely, are accepted as valid, then the rise of modern industry in America constitutes an unexplainable miracle. Free land was not exhausted in America until the close of the nineteenth century, and for at least a century and a half the tilled land of America was cultivated by the owners of one-family farms (except for the southern plantation system and a relatively small and scattered agricultural wage-laboring class). Pauperism had never existed in America in Marx's time on more than a local scale, or for brief periods of congestion of immigrants in the old industrial centers, or for that matter after Marx except for the 1929–33 economic crisis. Roosevelt's famous "one-third of the nation ill-housed, ill-clothed, and ill-fed" constituted an economic aristocracy in comparison with the poverty of Europe, and had no relation to Marx's "lazarus-layer" of a century before. The long-term American tendency has been for the wage scale to rise in proportion to production. The subsistence minimum has never represented more than a minor fraction of the whole wage, and has constantly become a smaller proportion.

America is exceptional, in the sense that these unconditional statements cannot be made about other countries except, in lesser degree, Canada, Australia, and New Zealand. All other lands in which the modern means of production have arisen, experienced mass pauperism for more or less prolonged periods, few of them have shown a long-term tendency for the wage level to keep pace with production, and the subsistence minimum has always played a larger role in determining wages than in America.

That means the rejected "laws" were not mere figments of imagination, whether of Marx or the other classical economists who preceded him with analogous doctrines; they were more or less valid generalizations of mass experience in most countries, with the emphatic exception of America. The American exception proves they were not "absolute general laws of capitalism," but leaves open a whole series of questions, for example, whether in other lands they are "laws" conditional on the presence of factors not to be found in America, such as a closed land monopoly.

Even for America, there have often been local and temporary examples of impoverishment similar to Europe's more general ones which gave birth to the rejected doctrines in the most brilliant minds of mankind. Indeed, while we must completely reject the disputed doctrines as explaining or compatible with the rise of modern industry in America, it must be admitted that this does not prove they would never find application should conditions change fundamentally, as, for example, through the destruction by atomic war. In other words, while we reject them as "absolute laws," we do not reject them "absolutely" as never, under all circumstances, having validity of some sort.

While these doctrines or dogmas of Marxism are no aid, but rather obstacles, to understanding the rise of American economy, the case is quite otherwise with the thought of

Marx with these dogmas set aside. We will find that Marx, minus the dogmas, is brilliantly illuminating for the whole problem.

At the opening of the nineteenth century America and England were roughly, by and large, operating economies of the same technological level. American agriculture enjoyed some advantages, due less to technology than to the comparative freedom of the soil from semi-feudal encumbrances and parceling, to the fact that the farmer was the proprietor of the land and working for his own benefit, and to the unexhausted virgin character of the soil. Its industry enjoyed the single but considerable advantage of a domestic market expanding more rapidly than its industry for a long time. But until America gained leadership in technology, its advance in international trade was slowed by the high wage level.

High wages were soon transformed, however, from a handicap into America's most decisive asset in all respects. All other factors in America's economic rise have their chief importance in so far as they contributed to maintaining the high level that originally arose from the free land system. It is hardly an exaggeration to say that for America it was high wages, rather than impoverishment, that was "the absolute general law" of capitalist accumulation.

This is a shocking and outrageous proposition, not only to the dogmatic Marxist; it is equally a heresy to conservative political economy. It was David Ricardo who, long before Marx, laid down the law that "when wages rise, profits fall," and that "profits depend on high or low wages, and on nothing else." James Mill expressed the same thought when he said that "profits depend wholly on wages." The thought persists among American economists, untainted by Marx, from Alexander Hamilton down to the present day. Whenever there is a disturbance in the economy, high wages are almost always listed high among the causes, and a dose of lower wages as the cure, whether the trouble be diagnosed as inflation, deflation, or what have you. Economists who disagree with such "fundamentalism" are timid about publicly expressing their views. Although in recent years there has been some boasting about American high wages, as a prestige item, they are not cited as a *cause* of prosperity but as a result, with wages as a *handicap* overcome only by the special genius of American entrepreneurs.

The trend of economic theory going to support the subsistence-wage theory and impoverishment is thus seen to embrace the political Right as well as Left, reactionaries and conservatives as well as dogmatic Marxists. It is not mitigated in its role as theory by those humanitarian expressions as to the social desirability of high wages which often, if not usually, accompanies economic theory tending to prove high wages are harmful to economic growth, as stimulating consumption at the expense of accumulation. Thus Ricardo, the most consistent and rigorous expounder of the subsistence-wage theory, in the midst of his treatise thereon comes forth with the most liberal expressions of the social desirability of high wages, opening a long paragraph to this effect with the statement:

> The friends of humanity cannot but wish that in all countries the laboring classes should have a taste for comforts and enjoyments, and that they should be stimulated by all legal means in their exertions to procure them. (Ricardo, *Principles,* etc., Everyman's Library, London and New York, p. 57.)

Similar statements are to be found in M'Culloch, James Mill, John Stuart Mill, and perhaps most, if not all, of the classical economists. I have heard these expressions quoted in discussions to prove that these economists did not stand on the subsistence-wage theory. But these statements are not economic theory, they are what lawyers would call *obiter dicta,* collateral expressions included in a judgment which are not, however, of any binding force in defining the law involved.

There was, of course, a basis of hard reality behind Ricardo and his formula, carried over and further developed by Marx, that "profits depend on high or low wages, and on nothing else." Marx put it, "what one gains, the other loses," and went on accurately to describe the attitude of the contestants:

> ... The continuous struggle between capital and labor [shows] the capitalist constantly tending to reduce wages to their physical minimum, and to extend the working day to its maximum, while the working man constantly presses in the opposite direction. (Marx, *Selected Works,* Vol. 1, p. 334.)

This is the way in which the issue appears to employers and workers, whether in England or America or any other country, from the beginning of capitalist relations down to the present day. And so far as concerns the *immediate* effect of the struggle, the appearance is true, and "what one gains, the other loses." But economic theory has the task to see further and deeper than the immediate combatants in economic conflict, whether they be bargainers in the market place of physical commodity exchange, or the two sides in the capital-labor struggle. When we go beyond the *immediate* to a *consequent* result, we will find that the capitalist who wins the immediate battles with labor loses in the long run of profits and accumulation, and the capitalist who habitually loses to labor (provided always, of course, he is not an exception but the general rule) finds himself in the fortunate position of gaining out of his own defeats. The law that "what one gains, the other loses" is found to be stood on its head. Let us trace in some detail how this worked out in America.

The condition Marx described as the consequence of free land, where the population grows more rapidly than elsewhere but the labor market remains always understocked, makes it possible for the laboring man to defeat the primitive urge of the capitalist toward a subsistence wage and maximum hours of labor. Thus in America no man was for long helpless before the greed of employers, for he could always sooner or later find escape to some form of self-employment, in the last analysis going onto the land and becoming an independent farmer. The despotism of capital, which depends upon a stagnant surplus population being ever renewed and increased, fell to pieces. Profits were relatively low and wages high. The wage worker became a very independent sort of fellow, meeting the employer on a basis of bargaining equality, or even with a superior position since the worker could get along without any employer if necessary, while an employer without workers loses all function in society.[1]

If the defeat of capital by labor on the wage issue had any effect in retarding capitalist accumulation, however, it was not for long. Even in the earlier stages of modern technology, when it did not yet require huge investments, the capitalist who had low-wage labor at his command was slow to adopt it, but where high wages prevailed the capitalist soon learned that new methods of production could turn high wages into

1 John Strachey goes much too far, however, when he says: "By taking up free land an American wage earner could at any time escape right out of the capitalist system." (*Contemporary Capitalism,* p. 128.) The point here is not any escape out of the capitalist system, which was impossible, but the new tendencies given to the evolution of that system. While escaping from the factory when necessary, the worker was imposing upon the system as a whole a new character, and changing the character of the factory itself. Furthermore, America more than any other land early involved almost the whole population in intimate relation with the capitalist world market, through commodity production. While I am very sympathetic to Strachey's main thesis, and will have occasion to quote some of his conclusions approvingly, I also find it necessary from time to time, as in this case, to file a dissent.

low unit costs. The capitalist without an industrial reserve army to draw on at will to expand production learned to expand with the same labor force through higher technology. And even before he learned these lessons, the capitalist learned to live with high wages when the alternative was to close his business for lack of labor. Marx compiled page on page of the wailing and gnashing of teeth of employers operating under such pressure. It was an excellent training school for American entrepreneurs.

Some elements of advanced economics were forcing themselves into the minds of men. Reading Marx, one can trace a transformation occurring in the Ricardian formula that "profits depend on high or low wages, and on nothing else." Gradually there emerges the new formula, arising out of experience and practice, which says that profits depend on dear or cheap labor, and that this is not the same thing as high or low wages, but indeed it is quite the opposite. High wages come to mean cheap labor costs, while low wages mean dear labor costs. This lesson arises from comparing one country with another, first of all. Marx quotes many brilliant flashes of insight into this process from his predecessors and from English factory inspectors, going back almost a century. Thus he finds in a treatise published in 1777, by James Anderson, the following:

> . . . Although the apparent price of labor is usually lower in poor countries, where the produce of the soil, and grain in general, is cheap; yet it is in fact for the most part really higher than in other countries: For it is not the wage that is given to the laborer per day that constitutes the real price of labor, although it is its apparent price. The real price is that which a certain quantity of work performed actually costs the employer; and considered in this light, labour is in almost all cases cheaper in rich countries than in those that are poorer, although the price of

grain and other provisions is usually much lower.... (Cited by Marx, *Capital,* p. 613.)

Here are a few more examples of how the recognition arose that high wages tend to result in cheap labor costs. Marx writes:

J. W. Cowell, member of the Factory Commission of 1833, after careful investigation of the spinning trade, came to the conclusion that "in England wages are virtually lower to the capitalist, though higher to the operative [worker] than on the Continent of Europe."... The English Factory Inspector, Alexander Redgrave, in his report of October 31, 1866, proves by comparative statistics with Continental states, that in spite of lower wages and much longer working time, Continental labor is, in proportion to the product, dearer than English. *(Ibid.,* pp. 613–14.)

And Marx dug out of the Minutes of the Royal Commission on Railways, 1867, this succinct little gem:

Labour being dearer in Ireland than it is in England... because wages are so much lower. *(Ibid.,* p. 613.)

Or we may quote the words of Marx himself that

By comparing article with article in the same country, and the commodities of different countries, I might show... that on the average the high-priced labor produces the low-priced, and the low-priced labor produces the high-priced commodities. (Marx, *Selected Works,* Vol. 1, p. 301.)

The rise of American technology to leading position in the world began to emerge as a major feature during the first decades of the nineteenth century. Engels, who was a textile manufacturer in Manchester, noticed this historic movement when he wrote:

The latest improvements for spinning and weaving cotton have come, almost all, from America, and Manchester has to adopt them. In industrial inventions of all kinds, America has distinctly taken the lead.

There is no need for the old legend about "a Yankee inventive genius" to explain this. Inventions by English and Continental workers had to be taken to America to find practical use. Marx noted:

> . . . The invention nowadays of machines in England that are used only in North America, just as in the sixteenth and seventeenth centuries, machines were invented in Germany to be used only in Holland, and just as many a French invention of the eighteenth century was exploited in England alone. (*Capital,* p. 429.)

In each such case it is the country of higher wages that is able to exploit inventions wherever they may have been made, and the countries of low wages that export their inventions for others to use. America took the lead in inventions because its wage level was twice that of the British, rising to more than two and one-third times by the middle of the nineteenth century, and to about three and one-third times in mid-twentieth century. Comparatively low wages in England discouraged the application of labor-saving machinery, while American high wages put a big premium on every technological advance.

David Ricardo, in a flash of intuitive genius, gave what was probably the first clear recognition of the process that was to revolutionize the world, when he wrote:

"Machinery and labor are in constant competition, and the former can frequently not be employed until labor rises." (David Ricardo, *Principles of Political Economy and Taxation,* Everyman's Library, London and New York, 3rd ed., p. 270.)

But Ricardo himself was not equipped to follow up his

great discovery and to unlock the doors to which it was a key. It was in America before all others that this principle was at work to upset the world balance of power. But Ricardo immediately drew the opposite conclusion, that in America there was the least chance of illustrating his newly-discovered principle. He wrote in the next paragraph:

> In America and many other countries, where the food of man is easily provided, there is not nearly such great temptation to employ machinery as in England, where food is high and costs much labor for its production.

Ricardo's obvious error here is very revealing of the true issue of theory with which we are wrestling. He was thoroughly familiar with prices on the world market, and knew that American food was flooding Europe where, as Engels wrote later, its "competition is shaking the very foundations of European landed property, large and small." His subsistence theory of wages told him that American cheap food was the infallible sign of low wages for that country. We thus received a classical example of the fundamental fallacy of the subsistence-wage theory, since American wages with cheap food were high and English wages with dear food were comparatively low.

It is not so easy, however, to explain why Marx handled these points in Ricardo as he did. He seized upon Ricardo's brilliant generalization on competition between labor and the machine as one of the steps whereby he moved outside the limitations of the subsistence theory in 1865. We will examine this in detail in the next chapter. At this point we are interested in the question: Why did Marx completely ignore Ricardo's obvious error about America being one of the most unlikely places for the introduction of machinery, and pass it over in silence?

Knowing that Marx was in general always eager to correct errors in the work of his great predecessors, there is only one possible explanation why he did not do so at this point. It was not from any awe of Ricardo's prestige, because he justifiably believed he understood the capitalist economy better than Ricardo and all previous economists; and sometimes he attacked with seeming ferocity—not always justly, for he could smell apologetics at times when there was merely failure to draw revolutionary conclusions. For example, he spoke witheringly of DeStutt de Tracy as "that fish-blooded bourgeois doctrinaire" because the Frenchman set forth the impoverishment doctrine without declaring that such a system must be overthrown. If De Tracy had proclaimed himself a revolutionary, he would presumably have ceased to be either fish-blooded, or bourgeois, or doctrinaire in Marx's eyes, although his doctrine would have remained as it was, closely parallel to Marx's doctrine of impoverishment.

The reason Marx failed to correct Ricardo's error on America and machinery must lie, in my opinion, in the fact that he had not himself clarified his views on the subsistence wage, and to criticize the obvious error he would involve himself in criticizing the more fundamental error which he still partly shared. He was not ready to settle accounts with the whole subsistence-wage theory, and therefore he let sleeping dogs lie.

In fact Marx built the whole theoretical foundation of *Capital* on the *assumption* that in the long run the subsistence wage was the law, and therefore all departures from it could be ignored, as deviations from the norm. For example, in his letter to Engels of April 2, 1858, giving a conspectus of his work, he specifically stated that in the first section, Capital in General, "in the whole of this section it is assumed that the wages of labour are constantly equal to the lowest level." (*Selected Correspondence,* p. 106.) In the same way, the doctrine of impoverishment, taken over from his predecessors, is an *assumption* underlying his whole study, and is "proved" only in the same manner as the subsistence wage, that is, examples are accumulated of results consistent with the assumptions, and it is indisputably established that *if the capitalist has his way* there is no other possible result.

But in fixing his theory Marx forgot his more realistic view, when facing the problems of the practical world, which he had expressed in these words:

> The *will* of the capitalist is certainly to take as much as possible. What we have to do is not to talk about his *will,* but to enquire into his *power,* the *limits of that power,* and the *character of those limits.* (Marx, *Selected Works,* Vol. 1, p. 286.)

Certainly in America the limits of the power of capital to control wages were more drastic and permanent in their effects than Marx conceived of in his dogmas which he had accepted from the classical economists.

In short, Marx judged America ambiguously, and failed to see that America established a bigger "room" for capitalist growth than was allowed for by his dogmas, not because he was a revolutionist in theory, and broke away from the established doctrines of political economy but, on the contrary, because he clung to too many of those doctrines. Where the established political economy said that it was necessary for capitalist accumulation that wages be driven down toward subsistence, Marx did not refute the theory but only placed the necessity of the worker against that of capital. Where the old doctrine declared that the people must be impoverished in order that "the nation" might become rich, Marx agreed this was true while the capitalist system remained, he only called for an end to the system. When Adam Smith wrote that in violent conflicts about wage rates, "taken as a whole, the master is always master," Marx quoted him as being correct. On all these, Marx was in error *because he shared the error of the old political economy.* Where Marx went outside the limits of the older school, he approached closer to the truth.

In America there was no possibility to doubt, even in Marx's time, that the capitalist was defeated on wages, and there was no general law or tendency to impoverishment. The nation and its people gained, of course, from the defeat of the capitalist. But what is more important for economic theory is that *the capitalist gained from his own defeat.* Labor's victory on wages gave to capitalist production and accumulation its greatest stimulus, and released it from the restrictive limits on its room for growth that were set by primitive social relations which the capitalist wished, but was unable, to preserve.

III.

MARX'S TWO WAGE THEORIES

UP TO THIS point we have focused attention upon America and its exceptional position, its contradictions with the Marxist theoretical formulation of the laws of capitalism, and the consequent ambiguity of Marx in dealing with America.

Now, in order to deepen our theoretical analysis, we need a different focus, namely, upon Marx's wage theory in general, or rather, as we intend to demonstrate, *Marx's two wage theories.* And strange as it may seem, America plays only a peripheral role in the emergence of his second wage theory, although it might have been expected that American high wages would be the starting point of such re-examination. As the event proved, that was not the case. At the risk of some repetition, we will now essay a rounded if brief review of the development of wage theory in Marx's writings.

Marx first entered the field of economics *per se,* with a work known as *Wage-Labour and Capital.* This study began as a series of lectures to the German Workers' Club in Brussels in 1847, and in 1849 it was elaborated into a series of articles in the *Neue Rheinische Zeitung* entitled "Lohnarbeit und Kapital." Its starting point was the upheavals culminating in 1848, the events of which Marx noted as

> ... The chief elements in which the European class struggle between bourgeoisie and working class came to a head and by

means of which we proved that every revolutionary upheaval, however remote from the class struggle its goal may appear to be, must fail until the revolutionary working class is victorious, that every social reform remains a utopia until the proletarian revolution and the feudalist counter-revolution take arms against one another in a *world war.* (Marx, *Selected Works,* Vol. 1, pp. 252–3.)

Marx thus began his economic studies under the influence of events on the Continent, where feudal counterrevolution had triumphed over *the bourgeoisie and the workers,* primarily because the capital-labor contradiction split the anti-feudalist camp. *Wage-Labour and Capital* was conceived as the first part of a three-part study. The other parts were not published, were probably not written, but Marx's projection of what they were to be throws additional light on the work. He describes the unpublished parts thus:

2) *The inevitable downfall of the middle bourgeois classes and of the so-called peasant class under the present system,* 3) *the commercial subjugation and exploitation of the bourgeois classes of the various European nations* by the despot of the world market–*England.* (*Ibid.,* p. 253.)

In the thirty book pages of this study of capital-labor relationships, Marx's exuberant intellectual genius is already apparent, in his elaboration of the Ricardian subsistence-wage theory far beyond anything Ricardo attempted—but never overstepping its boundaries as set by Ricardo. Marx here sums up that theory as follows:

The cost of production of simple labour, therefore, amounts to the *cost of the existence and reproduction of the worker.* The price of this cost of existence and reproduction constitutes wages. Wages so determined are called the *wage minimum.* This wage minimum, like the determination of the price of commodities by the cost of production in general, does not hold good for the *single individual* but for the *species*. Individual workers, millions of workers, do not get enough to be able to exist and reproduce themselves; *but the wages of the whole working class* level themselves out within their variations to this minimum. (*Ibid.*, p. 263.)

Marx sums up, almost in the exact words of Ricardo, that "Profit rises to the extent that wages fall; it falls to the extent that wages rise."

Concerning the influence of the introduction of machinery on the course of wages, Marx writes:

> *The greater the expansion of division of labor and application of machinery, the greater is the expansion of competition among the workers, the greater is the contraction of their wages.* (*Ibid.*, p. 280.)

In Marx's correspondence outside his main theoretical works one may find occasional expressions that seem to forecast modifications of this theory to come later in 1865. Thus even before *Wage-Labour and Capital* was begun, Marx wrote in the course of a long letter to Annenkov on Proudhon (December 28, 1846) that "it is only true of England" that the invention and application of machinery were the result of the war between workers and employers, while the Continent was "driven" to it by English competition, and in America he ascribes "lack of hands" as a major motive. Such examples are important, as evidence of recognition of facts, but do not yet constitute even an embryonic or incomplete theory for dealing with the facts.

In 1859, Marx made his only well-defined and finished revision of Ricardo's wage theory. This had to do, however, not with subsistence as the controlling norm for wages, which is the essential point of our present study, but with the definition of the commodity which the laborer brings to the market. Marx had been satisfied until then with the Ricardian formula that wages were the price of labor. But in working out his book *Zur Kritik der Politischen Œkonomie,* first complete outline of his major economic theories, published in 1859, some eight years before *Capital,* Vol. 1, appeared, Marx found in this formula a logical stumbling block to deepening his analysis, and therefore revised it to distinguish between labor, creator of value and therefore outside the category of price, and labor power or capacity to labor, the commodity which the laborer brings to the market and for which he receives a wage.

We need not now delve into the significance of this revision, for it does not affect the present study. Under it, subsistence plays exactly the same role as under the original Ricardian formula. The two phases of Marx's utilization of the Ricardian law, before and after 1859, are dealt with here as a single theory, and are not the "two wage theories" of which we speak.

Until 1865, I know of no example of Marx using a wage theory that goes beyond the limits of the subsistence norm as the controlling factor in the long run. Marx did energetically combat Ferdinand Lassalle's "iron law of wages" which is often confused with Ricardo's theory. But Ricardo, for all the rigorousness with which he defined "subsistence," did not see it as *immediately* determining wages as in the "iron law," or as precluding deviations above subsistence, and even less did Marx, whose definition was more flexible than Ricardo's.[1]

[1] William J. Blake, in *An American Looks at Karl Marx,* for example, is confused when he writes that Lassalle was "a direct follower of Ricardo" and got his "iron law of wages" from him (p. 628). Even such a competent man as John Strachey speaks of the "iron law" as a "very natural conclusion" from Marx (*Contemporary Capitalism,* p. 123). And the reputable Isaiah Berlin writes in *Foreign Affairs* (October 1957, p. 19) as though the "iron law" was the direct creation of Marx when he speaks of "such stock Marxist categories as capitalist exploitation, the iron law of wages" . . . etc. Such failures to distinguish between Lassalle, Ricardo, and Marx, on this question, while widespread, are not justified by a careful reading of their works. The "iron law" was a vulgarized, corrupted version of the subsistence-wage theory.

Therefore we cannot, despite confusions on the question in reputable quarters, interpret Marx's assault on the "iron law" as being by itself a step outside the subsistence theory.

But Marx did take such a step in 1865. It has been read by millions of students without, so far as I am aware, it being recognized as a new stage in Marx's theory of wages—probably because Marx himself did not publicly so recognize it.

The occasion was a report by Marx to the General Council of the International Workingmen's Association, on June 20 and 27, 1865. Marx had undertaken to answer and refute an earlier report by Weston, another member of the Council, who had defended the thesis that wage increases do not improve the social and material prospects of the working class (a version of the "iron law" of Lassalle and identical with Daniel DeLeon's later interpretation of Marx in America). Marx set himself the task to defend the role and purpose of trade-unions, and prove theoretically their ability to improve the situation of the working class in more than a superficial and temporary sense. He did a masterful job of it, and produced what will no doubt live in history as a "classic." Considering its pioneering character, and the general state of economic science, it was a work of genius, no matter how much, in the light of a century of experience and thought, we may now see it as inadequate and even contradictory.

Marx had only one month in which to prepare this report. At first he took the task lightly, writing to Engels that rather than interrupt his work on *Capital,* he would rely on "improvisation." But the magnitude of the issue obviously prevailed upon him to prepare a manuscript of some fifty-six book pages. It is remarkable, considering his first offhand approach, that it represents one of his most revolutionary and original contributions to economic theory.

It is clear that Marx found, in his preparations for the

debate, that the subsistence-wage theory loomed up more and more as an embarrassment.[2] The situation drove him to think fast and deep, as no consideration of theory had driven him in his more planned work, and he met it with his own original contribution to wage theory which was not an elaboration of Ricardo, but which stepped boldly outside the limitations of the subsistence wage. This original contribution finds its essence in the following paragraph:

> Besides this mere physical element [subsistence], the value of labor is in every country determined by a *traditional standard of life.* It is not mere physical life, but it is the satisfaction of certain wants springing from the social conditions. . . . This historical or social element, entering into the value of labor, may be expanded or contracted, or altogether extinguished, so that nothing remains but the physical *limit.* . . . The *value of labor* itself is not a fixed but a variable magnitude, even supposing the value of all other commodities to remain constant.[3] (Marx, *Selected Works,* Vol. 1, pp. 332–3.)

What is new in principle here, in basic theory, is not the recognition that tradition and habit make for resisting wage cuts and thereby maintaining wages above subsistence. Ricardo himself recognized such influences upon the actual course of wages, but considered them as deviations above value, as did Marx until he formulated this report. Here he

[2] Marx wrote to Engels that it is "not easy to explain to ignorant people all the economic questions which compete with one another here. *You can't compress a course of political economy in one hour. But we shall do our best.*" In the event he devoted not one hour but two whole evenings to his report. See *Selected Correspondence,* p. 202.

[3] It is of interest to note here that Marx freely used the formula "value of labor," rather than "value of labor power," which was his correction to Ricardo and upon which he and Engels placed great emphasis, although this was six years after he had made that correction. Obviously his audience was more habituated to the former expression, and would understand either one in the same sense, because in the context the correction carried no significance.

broke decisively with the Ricardian theory, and admitted a social increment above subsistence as "entering into the value of labor," not merely into the wage or price. Here is further the recognition of that value as *variable* independently of any relationship with other commodities. This is the complete abandonment in principle of subsistence as the determining norm for the value of labor power and thereby, in the long run, for wages.

Where the subsistence-wage theory says "the value of labor power is settled like that of every other commodity," and that it "resolves itself into the value of a definite quantity of the means of subsistence and varies with the value of those means," the new theory of Marx says, on the contrary, that there is a *distinction in principle* between the value of labor power and every other commodity, that it is a magnitude that is variable even when that of the means of subsistence remains constant. Where the subsistence theory is thus named because it says that subsistence furnishes the norm for wages, with deviations above that norm being departures from value, the new theory reduces subsistence to a mere *lower limit* below which that value cannot fall but above which it may rise indefinitely, so that ". . . although we can fix the *minimum* of wages, we cannot fix their *maximum*." Where the subsistence theory is essentially Ricardo's, with Marx contributing only a deeper analysis and logical corrections in precise formulation, the new theory is an advance in principle beyond Ricardo that belongs to Marx alone.

Marx's report to the General Council was approved, and a motion was passed calling for its publication. Marx wrote to Engels:

> Now the people want to have this printed. . . . In the second part the thing contains, in an extremely condensed but relatively popular form, much that is new, taken in advance from my book,

while at the same time it has necessarily to slur over all sorts of things. (*Selected Correspondence,* p. 203.)

But as it turned out the report was not to be printed for a third of a century. And what was new on wage theory in the report was not more fully elaborated in *Capital,* but only registered there in its most generalized form, with supporting material not organized but scattered under other headings, and what was new was not emphasized but "slurred over."

If there was any further correspondence between Marx and Engels on this report, it has not been published in English to my knowledge. However that may be, the report itself was not published during Marx's lifetime. With Marx's death, his manuscripts passed into the hands of Engels as his literary executor, but still the report was not published.

In 1891, the German Social-Democratic party decided to publish ten thousand copies of Marx's study of wages in a pamphlet for the education of its members, and appealed to Engels to edit such a pamphlet. The record is not clear on this point, but since in 1884 the party had published *Wage-Labour and Capital* in its original form, it was probably suggested that this be reissued. At any rate, that is what was done, whether on the initiative of the party or of Engels, who wrote a long introduction for it. Here Engels explains some changes he made in the original text, saying, "Marx would certainly have brought the old presentation dating from 1849 into harmony with his new point of view." He continued: "I therefore tell the reader beforehand: this is not the pamphlet as Marx wrote it in 1849 but approximately as he would have written it in 1891."

But the changes Engels introduced "all turn on one point. According to the original, the worker sells his *labor* to the capitalist for wages; according to the present text he sells his labor *power.*" That is all. The subsistence-wage theory of

1849 is reproduced without change. There is not even a mention of the unpublished report to the General Council of the International Workingmen's Association in 1865, or of the completely new theory there set forth or its inclusion in principle in *Capital.* (See Engels, Introduction to *Wage-Labour and Capital, Selected Works,* Vol. 1, pp. 242-51.)

When Engels died in 1895, Marx's manuscripts came into the hands of Eleanor Aveling, Marx's daughter, who found the report among them and caused it to be published in 1898, as the pamphlet known under the title *Value, Price and Profit.*

One can only speculate as to the reasons for the thirty-three years' delay in publication. That the delay was unfortunate is beyond doubt. For during that one-third of a century the dogmatic interpretation of Marx on wages in the pure Ricardian sense became fixed, and became a vested interest among Marx's rapidly growing body of disciples, among whom dogmatism grew to such rigidity as to cause Marx himself to exclaim in disgust: "I am not a Marxist!"

The words of Engels in 1891, quoted above, carry the clear meaning by implication that Marx had repudiated the new theory contained in the 1865 report to the General Council, and would not have repeated it in 1891 had he lived. I find myself unable to believe that this was the case. And since I cannot believe that Engels was deliberately concealing anything, I cannot come to any other conclusion but that he did not understand the issues that were involved, or he would have written frankly about them.

The chief evidence that Engels was wrong in saying that *Wage-Labour and Capital* represented Marx's final word on wage theory, and that he had abandoned the new theory set forth in *Value, Price and Profit,* is the fact that *Marx included the essential features of the new theory in Capital,* published two years after the report to the General Council, even if without the fuller development contained in the original report. This may be found on page 190, in a paragraph that reads:

> ... The number and extent of [the worker's] so-called necessary wants, as also the modes of satisfying them, are themselves the product of historical development, and depend therefore to a great extent on the degree of civilization of a country, more particularly on the habits and degree of comfort in which the class of free laborers has been formed. In contradistinction therefore to the case of other commodities, there enters into the determination of the value of labor power a historical and moral element.

This paragraph containing in principle all the elements of the new theory is, however, presented simultaneously with the subsistence theory (for example, on p. 191, following immediately after the above), without any attempt to harmonize them, and with no formal recognition of the conflict between them. These things suggest that Marx seriously held the new theory but had not yet settled accounts with the old one. The issue represented "unfinished business" for him which he never got around to completing. And because Marx had not finished it, Engels, who took no initiative in this field whatever, was glad to forget it and probably really did.

Marx's failure to announce the new theory as such, or even to complete its formulation, and his refusal to publish the original report, are doubtless responsible for the fact that the new wage theory does not have a name to distinguish it from the old theory. My own fifty years of reading and study in Marxist and anti-Marxist literature have brought to my attention not a single book where the existence of *two wage theories in Marx* was recognized and discussed. Yet the fact is so clear and indisputable, whatever the merits of the two theories, that one cannot continue the silence that has reigned on the question for almost a century.[4] Since we have in this study recognized the new theory in its own right, established its distinct identity and ancestry, and will later demonstrate examples of how Marx applied it with notable results that could not have been reached with the old theory, it would seem to be appropriate to pause a moment to christen the new theory with a name of its own. My suggestion would be to call it the *social-wage theory*.

Like most of Marx's original contributions, his new theory does not *abolish* the old, but rather *incorporates* it into a new synthesis, where the old takes on new meanings and, while being subordinated to the new, is also raised by it to a higher theoretical level. The old theory is still valid in the rare situation where capital is able to establish its despotism over wages. In the social-wage theory, subsistence does not disappear as a factor, but its role is changed from *determinate norm* to *floor or base,* above which there is a variable social increment.

The old theory of the subsistence wage emphasized the basic confrontation of employer versus worker, of capital versus labor, and on the *assumption* that this takes place within a social context overwhelmingly favorable to capital and unfavorable to labor, traces the consequences as the fixing of wages around the norm of subsistence. The result is already predetermined in the assumption from which the

[4] I have heard reports, without seeing any documents to support them, that the Marx-Engels Institute in Moscow discussed this problem, and rejected the view that *Value, Price and Profit* should not be recognized as an authentic part of Marxism on the grounds of Marx's failure to publish it and Engels' declaration of 1891 that *Wage-Labour and Capital* represented Marx's wage theory "as he would have written it in 1891" with the single correction that "labor power" is substituted for "labor." Whatever may be the facts about unpublished discussions, the issue has been systematically kept out of the authorized textbooks on Marxist economic theory.

examination started. The new theory shows that the assumption is rarely more than an approximation, and is often a radical departure from reality, that the social context may contain a wide range of factors favorable to labor in this confrontation and, therefore, the consequence may be, and often if not usually is, a wage fixed in some degree *above* subsistence, and even so much above as to reduce subsistence to a minor factor in wages, and to inaugurate a self-movement of the economy toward higher levels. "The question resolves itself into a question of the respective powers of the combatants," as Marx said repeatedly.

The value of labor power is a function of the whole social context, and not a function of the subsistence level, which merely sets a natural limit to any downward movement, as total net production is a natural limit on the upward movement. The distinction between labor power and all other commodities lies in the fact that value in the latter expresses the quantitative relations in the distribution of labor among the various fields of economic activity, while in the former it expresses the relation of labor to society as a whole.

The *increment above subsistence* contained in the value of labor power is a measure of the degree of material civilization to which a given society has achieved. It is the historical, social, or moral element in the value of labor power, which serves not only as a *measure* of progress, but is an *instrument* of progress, inasmuch as it acts, to a degree that rises with its relative volume, as a stimulus to increased productivity through higher technology. The dynamic relationship between these factors does not run on the line that higher technology, through increased productivity, produces high wages, but on the contrary line that higher wages, by stimulating higher technology, expands productivity and accumulation.

Where the subsistence-wage theory said: "The value of labor power resolves itself into the value of a definite quantity of the means of subsistence," we may change this into the social-wage theory without striking out a single word, but merely by adding: "Plus a historical, social, or moral element which measures the degree of material civilization of the given society, and furnishes the motive-force of economic progress."

The social-wage theory closes the abyss that for so long separated Marxism from the American labor movement and from American experience in general. In America the social increment above subsistence in wages was always obvious as the major factor, and therefore the insistence of early American socialists upon a dogmatic subsistence-wage theory (or even upon the "iron law" in the case of DeLeon and the Lassalleans) drove the American labor movement away from Marxism and away from all theory. The labor movement in America, and to a somewhat lesser degree in England, simply could not accept an economic theory that explained high wages as a deviation from value or "natural price," and therefore doomed to attrition from the normal action of the law of value. The social-wage theory explains the social increment above subsistence as a constituent part of value of labor power, with economic consequences upon production as a whole that lead, not to attrition of high wages downward but, on the contrary, stimulation of wages toward higher levels.

Why did not American high wages stimulate Marx to the conclusions of the social-wage theory? Probably because he had a blanket formula to explain the special conditions of America as the result of *lack of development* as a capitalist economy, and he never realized the utter inadequacy of this formula. How did he come to realize the social-wage theory on the basis of English facts, even though English wages were less than half the American level? Unquestionably it was because the International Workingmen's Association to which he made the report was composed in the main of English trade-unions. Marx himself, in a letter to Engels announcing that he was going to make the report, commented that if the General Council accepted Weston's thesis "we should be turned into a joke both on account of the trade-unions here and of the *infection of strikes* which now prevails on the Continent." (*Selected Correspondence,* p. 202.)

The danger "that we should be turned into a joke" was what stimulated Marx to re-examine his old wage theory. And as he faced this danger, he realized that it was impossible to make a reasoned defense of the trade-unions on a long-term basis within the limitations of the subsistence-wage theory, which he himself sixteen years earlier had explained to mean that "individual workers, millions of workers, do not get enough to be able to exist and reproduce themselves, *but the wages of the whole working class* level themselves out within their variations to this minimum." Old Weston, the carpenter, who knew almost nothing of economics except some current slogans and catch phrases, had put the greatest economist of his time *on the spot* and forced him to recast his theories.

What made it *possible* for Marx to come up with the social-wage theory to meet this emergency was, of course, something else again. When forced seriously to re-examine the question, Marx found within his own analyses of detailed economic problems, as he had already worked them out, all the elements of the social-wage theory which *only had to be assembled* and directed toward this new focus in order to give the new answers. He simply had not faced the necessity to do so before.

Finally, we must try to understand why the social-wage

theory, then and for his whole life, remained *unfinished business* for Marx. We have already noted that in refusing to publish his report in 1865, he explained that *Capital,* to appear in 1867, would deal with the question more completely and adequately. There was, indeed, ample ground for wishing to improve the report, for even though it was a historical advance of supreme importance, it remained full of unresolved contradictions, and what was new in it was not *pointed out* as a higher stage of theory, subordinating the old theory of *Wage-Labour and Capital.* But when *Capital* appeared, all that it contained directly from the new theory was one paragraph (page 190) giving a condensed summary of the thought, and elements of the social-wage analysis appear only in scattered form. The whole volume is founded on the assumption that he announced in 1858 that "... it is assumed that the wages of labor are constantly at their lowest level." Thus by omission *Capital,* in so far as wage theory is concerned, represents a step backward from *Value, Price and Profit,* which was not published until thirty-three years after it was written and thirty-one years after *Capital* was published. This could only have been because Marx was beginning to break under the strain of his troubles, prolonged poverty, and sickness.

Marx is unquestionably the father of the social-wage theory, but he treated the child very badly, not at all as he behaved toward his flesh-and-blood children, in which relation he was the traditional doting father. Toward this, one of his most important brain children, he behaved more as Lord Byron toward his "little bastard" Allegra, permitting, by his neglect, the dogmatists to bury it in nearly a century of obscurity.

IV.

AMERICA, ENGLAND, AND THE SOCIAL WAGE

AMERICA presents the outstanding example of the social wage, with the increment above subsistence far higher than any other country. Yet Marx developed the social-wage analysis with only incidental reference to America, and depended mainly on English experience. Whatever the reason for this, it shows that while America's exceptional conditions gave it the higher relative position, the principles of the social wage were equally operative in England within the limits of historical circumstances. The laws and principles of capitalist economy remain uniform, but their results differ according to the circumstances of the various countries.

The comparison between America and England gives us many insights into the thought of Marx. The two countries differed first, and most sharply, in the contrast between free land in America and closed land monopoly in England. That is why the former was marked by scarcity of hands and consequent high wages, and the latter by a stagnant surplus population and comparatively low wages.

If America had this advantage over England, however, we must note that England held a similar advantage over the Continent. Even as America stood above England in wages and general welfare in the first half of the nineteenth century, so also did England stand above the capitalist economies of continental Europe and in about the same ratio. As American production under a wage scale more than twice that of England could undersell that country's products on the world market, so also could the English, with a wage scale similarly above that of Europe, undersell the continental products.

In America the starting point was high wages on the basis of free land. In England, where there was no free land, how did this principle of higher wages, stimulating technology, come into operation?

Engels, whose talents lay more in historical than economic analysis, was nevertheless the first to suggest that the earlier rise of England over the Continent was due to the same principles that brought the later rise of America over England. Writing in *The Labour Standard* of June 18, 1881, he said:

> There is no mistake about it, the present generation will see American cotton goods compete with English ones in India and China, and gradually gain ground in these two leading markets; American machinery and hardware compete with the English markets in all parts of the world, England included; and the same implacable necessity which removed Flemish manufactures to Holland, Dutch ones to England, will ere long remove the center of the world's industry from this country to the United States.

There is little doubt that Engels' intuitive insight into this question is sound, although much study and research are still required to demonstrate with concrete evidence just how the process worked in each case, just what were the differences and what were the common principles at work. But Marx already established in principle, in his report to the General Council in 1865, that it was the rising role of labor that raised and kept England above the Continent. He found in the English Factory Acts, characteristic feature of the higher effectiveness of English democracy as compared with the Continent, and their resulting effect on the English economy, a factor that released some of the principles of growth in England, even if on a lower scale, as the factor of free land had released them in America. In this analysis Marx had to overcome his own prejudice that "every social reform remains a utopia until the proletarian revolution," and no critic could be more harsh and ruthless than was Marx in exposing the inadequacy of the Factory Acts, the blind greed of English employers in opposing them, the servility of government and courts in conniving at their violation, and so on. Yet Marx, as no other writer of the time, analyzed clearly the profound changes that were introduced into the English economy by the Factory Acts, all of which exemplified the principles of the social wage. In his report to the General Council, Marx wrote:

> You are all aware of the Ten Hours Bill . . . introduced since 1848. This was one of the greatest economic changes we have witnessed. It was a sudden and compulsory rise in wages, not in some local trades, but in the leading industrial branches by which England sways the markets of the world. . . . All the official mouthpieces of the middle class *proved* . . . that it would sound the death-knell of English industry. They proved that it not only amounted to a simple rise of wages, but to a rise of wages initiated by, and based upon, a diminution of the quantity of labor employed. . . . They threatened a decrease of accumulation, rise of prices, loss of markets, stinting of production, consequent reaction upon wages, ultimate ruin. . . . Well, what was the result? A rise in money wages of the factory operatives, despite the curtailment of the working day, a great increase in the number of factory hands employed, a continuous fall in the price of their products, a marvellous development in the productive powers of their labor, an unheard-of progressive expansion of the markets for their commodities. (Marx, *Selected Works,* Vol. 1, p. 291.)

Further on in the same report Marx discusses how every rise in the status of the workers stimulates production and productivity, and benefits capital as well, and brings in Ricardo's principle of competition between men and machines. He writes:

> In colonial countries the law of supply and demand favors the workingman. Hence the relatively high standard of wages in the United States. Capital may there try its utmost. It cannot prevent the labour market from being continuously emptied by the continuous conversion of wages laborers into independent, self-sustaining peasants. . . . But let us now come to old civilized countries, in which capital domineers over the whole process of production. Take, for example, the rise in England of agricultural wages from 1849 to 1859. What was its consequences? The farmers could not . . . raise the value of wheat, nor even its market prices. They had, on the contrary, to submit to their fall. But during these eleven years they introduced machinery of all sorts, adopted more scientific methods, converted part of the arable land into pasture, increased the size of farms and with this the scale of production, and by these and other processes diminishing the demand for labor by increasing its productive power, made the agricultural laborer again relatively redundant. This is the general method in which a reaction, quicker or slower, of capital against a rise of wages takes place in old settled countries. Ricardo has justly remarked that machinery is in constant competition with labor, and can often be only introduced when the price of labor has reached a certain height, but the appliance of machinery is but one of the many methods for increasing the productive powers of labor. (Marx, *Selected Works,* Vol. 1, pp. 334–5.)

In these quotations from Marx we have the analytical elements of a rounded social-wage theory. These are: the recognition that a rise in wages, however it may be produced, has the *immediate* result to lower profits but the *consequent* result to increase the productivity of labor and thereby increase accumulation; that the improvement of the status of labor is thus a condition to the rise of the volume of profits to a new high level; that both these results arise from the premium that high wages place upon the introduction of machinery and technological improvements in general, especially the most expensive. Here Marx was depending entirely on English experience, much narrower in its significance than the American, which he left to one side as "exceptional" and requiring special treatment. But even in England it is learned that increasing wages adds to the growth and stability of the entire economy, which even to the capitalist may be more important than immediate profits.

Let me be quite clear that I claim for Marx *only the production of all the elements of a rounded social-wage theory*. After 1865 he did not further develop and apply the theory, he did not even publish his report, he did not, as he had promised, incorporate in *Capital* the materials of his report in improved and completed form, but only its general principles, he did not settle the problem of a synthesis of the two conflicting theories with subsistence subordinated to social increment, he did not define the results of his new theory on his over-all theoretical system. The new theory remained for Marx "unfinished business."

Disregarding for the moment the obvious and surface contradictions contained in *Value, Price and Profit,* we may go deeper into the theoretical issues that stood as a block between Marx and the completion of the social-wage theory. Toward the end of the report, Marx said:

> "With the development of the productive powers of labour the accumulation of capital will be accelerated, even despite a relatively high rate of wages." (*Ibid.,* p. 335.)

Here Marx had recoiled from the line of thought that produced the social-wage theory, back to the Ricardian dogma that "what one gains, the other loses." After showing not only that rising wages resulted in increased production, but was a necessary precondition thereto in its more advanced forms; that this step results in accelerated accumulation and expanded profits; Marx then returns to the first step in the process and says that what followed was not because of this first step, but despite it. Again we are faced with the ever-recurring conflict in Marx between scientific observation and analysis on one hand, and dogmatic predetermination of final conclusions on the other hand.

It would be a gross oversimplification of our problem to interpret this in the petty and superficial sense of a breakdown in logic. Marx was the one man least likely of all to be tripped up by mere logical complexities. For him logic was always instrument and never master. He was not timid in face of contradictions, and understood the union of incompatibles as something to be met without surprise in all fields. This problem was not on the plane of logic. It was the contradiction between the machine made possible by high wages, and that same machine in its role of rendering the laborer redundant. It was, in last analysis, the problem of what happens to the working class when the machine has finally replaced, say, 90 per cent of the workers' functions. Marx failed to conceive of this contradiction as a process of partial resolution and constant reappearance on a higher level, in a rising cycle of economic advance, with each phase of the cycle finding its impetus in the rising social and political stature of labor, based on but not limited to its economic status. He could only conclude, as he did even in the report defending the trade-unions, that:

> ...The very development of modern industry must progressively turn the scale in favor of the capitalist against the workingman, and that consequently the general tendency of capitalist pro-

duction is not to raise, but to sink the average standard of wages, or to push the *value of labor* more or less to its *minimum limit.* (*Ibid.*, p. 336.)

It is on the ground of historical evidence that this dogma must be refuted, and not on grounds of logic. For this it is not necessary to appeal to the evidence since Marx, but may be done with evidence taken from Marx himself. The refutation is contained in the comparison of America, England, and the Continent.

Marx himself tells us that the relative wage levels of these three areas in the mid-nineteenth century were roughly as 4, 2, and 1. No matter how much Marx explains that the American figure of 4 is due to exceptional conditions that do not hold in the "old societies" where capitalism first grew to modern proportions (and this is valid as to the origin of the high American level), this still does not explain how America with that high wage level could under his "general tendency of capitalist production" overtake and surpass England in such capitalist production without depressing, but on the contrary raising further, its wage level. Nor does it explain how England, once inferior to continental capitalist countries, rose to world dominance to the accompaniment of a wage level twice as high as that of the Continent. If the development of modern industry "must progressively turn the scale in favor of the capitalist against the workingman," then the country with the most modern industry would also have the closest approximation to the subsistence wage, or at least some approximation of that condition. The fact that the American wage level represented by 4, the English by 2, and the Continent by 1, corresponds more to their relative stature in modern industry than it does the reverse, proves that there is a false link in Marx's chain of reasoning, and that false link is the assumption that the power of the capitalist increases with the growth of modern industry.

As for the American 4, Marx frankly admitted that it is explained by the fact that capital was unable to establish its "despotism" over wages. The English 2 means that capital had more despotic powers in England than in America. By the same token, then, the continental 1 means that capital on the Continent had more despotic powers than in England. But this order of capitalist power does not show that the scale is being turned in favor of the capitalist and against the worker by the development of modern industry, but rather the opposite. The most undeveloped in modern industry have the lower wage level, and the higher developed have the higher wage level. The weaker is the capitalist economy, the stronger is capital in dictating wages; the stronger is the capitalist economy, the weaker is capital as against labor on the wages question. The coincidence of fact is obvious and unescapable. There remains, however, to consider Marx's judgment that America was "undeveloped" in the capitalist sense, and what this means to our problem.

We must ask ourselves, first, what was Marx's exact meaning when he judged America was undeveloped. He *did not* mean that modern industry was absent, or that it was inferior in quality to the English. Nor did he mean that the American economy was not capitalist, although there are indications in his earlier writings that he toyed with this idea.[1]

[1] For example, Marx wrote (*Theorien uber den Mehrwert,* Vol. II-2, pp. 70–72) that "in colonies like the United States and Australia, the mass of farming colonists are not capitalists and their production is not capitalist even though they bring more or less capital with them from the old country. They are farmers who work more or less for themselves, who are primarily engaged in the production of the necessities of life for their own existence. Thus their main products are not commodities and are not destined for the market." Later, however, Marx and Engels fully recognized that at least by the time of the Revolution, American economy was one of commodity production, even in agriculture, more fully than any other country except,

What was "undeveloped" then about American capitalism? Unquestionably Marx had chiefly in mind the American high wages and living standards, the absence of a stagnant surplus population such as that in England and on the Continent, and the consequent absence of low wages and impoverishment which for him were among the dominant signs of "development" in capitalism. Above all, America had a free land system, operative until long after Marx's death, and he considered the expropriation of the masses from the land as the very foundation of capitalist production. These were Marx's grounds for calling America "undeveloped."

But these very peculiarities of America were primarily the signs of *the absence of remnants of feudalism,* rather than the lack of development of capitalism. As Engels expressed it in a letter to an American friend (Florence Kelly Wischnewetsky) on June 3, 1886:

> For America after all was the ideal of all bourgeois; a country *rich, vast, expanding,* with purely *bourgeois* institutions unleavened by feudal remnants or monarchical traditions and without a permanent and hereditary proletariate. Here everyone could become, if not capitalist, at all events an independent man, producing or trading, with his own means, for his own account. (*Selected Correspondence,* p. 449.)

If America "was the ideal of all bourgeois," how then could it be considered an undeveloped capitalism, when capitalism is itself the more general "ideal of all bourgeois"?

On the general question of the relation between feudalism and capitalism, Marx was a model of clarity and precision,

---

perhaps, England. Their dominant concept from the late 1850's on was expressed by Engels when he wrote that "the United States are modern, bourgeois from the very origin; . . . they were founded by *petits* bourgeois and peasants who ran away from European feudalism to establish a purely bourgeois society." (Engels to Danielson, October 17, 1893, *Selected Correspondence,* p. 514.)

and far superior to all other contemporary economists. He saw clearly that the "old order" of social status inherited from feudalism was incompatible with the new civilization emerging from the modern means of production. His most devastating criticism of the new industrial bourgeoisie was that, out of fear of the rising social power of the working class which would break its despotism over wages, it betrayed its own historical role, came to terms with the remnants of feudalism, and halted the bourgeois revolution while it was still incomplete. He also recognized that in America there were the least remnants of feudalism.

Yet Marx never drew the obvious conclusion from these facts, that *the despotism of capital over wages is the consequence of semi-feudal remnants rather than of the "pure" conditions of a capitalist economy.*

When we find Marx contrasting the "normal" or "mature" capitalism of England with the "undeveloped" capitalism of America, therefore, we discover within this comparison the anomaly that the "signs of maturity" are closely connected with the feudal remnants incorporated into capitalist society by the failure of the bourgeoisie to complete its revolution; while the signs of America's "undeveloped" condition arise from the absence of such semi-feudal remnants. Thus Marx is seen to have accepted as a necessary part of "normal" capitalism its amalgamation with the remnants of feudal institutions and practices, and to have taken the absence of such an amalgamation as the mark of "undevelopment."

It was, however, impossible that America should *ever* become "developed" in this sense, for in America such small semi-feudal remnants that did exist before the Revolution were wiped out in its course and immediately after. In America the bourgeois revolution was not compromised, with the exception previously noted of slavery in the South and its remnants after the Civil War. And precisely this exception goes to prove our thesis, also, because in the South where there was a sort of amalgamation of bourgeois with pre-bourgeois society in some way analogous to the general conditions of Europe, precisely there was capitalism really and seriously *undeveloped,* and only in the last generation has modern industrialization taken charge.

America as a whole, however, the North and West especially, did develop but not on the English or European model. It took a different direction, that of unfolding the social wage and its consequence of a *higher type of capitalism* with a bigger room for the productive forces to expand, and a longer life expectancy than the European type—*even if all other features of the Marxist analysis of capitalism are taken as valid.* For as Marx said in his Preface to *Zur Kritik,* and the complete validity of this cannot be questioned, no social order ever disappears before all the productive forces for which there is room in it have developed, and higher relations of production do not appear until their material prerequisites have matured in the old society itself.

We are back, after a tour of some critical points in Marx's thought, to his assumption, quoted in the beginning of this study, that the countries most advanced industrially show to the less advanced the image of their own future. The element of truth contained in this aphorism serves very effectively to hide a profound fallacy which is responsible for Marx's mistakes about America. But this remains a complex question that calls for further analysis. I approach this task now by an extended quotation from the first pages of the Author's Preface to the First Edition of *Capital.* Marx wrote:

> The physicist either observes physical phenomena where they occur in their most typical form and most free from disturbing influences, or, wherever possible, he makes experiments under

conditions that assure the occurrence of the phenomena in its normality. In this work I have to examine the capitalist mode of production, and the conditions of production and exchange corresponding to that mode. Up to the present time, their classic ground is England. That is the reason why England is used as the chief illustration in the development of my theoretical ideas. If, however, the German reader shrugs his shoulders at the conditions of the English industrial and agricultural labourers, or in optimistic fashion comforts himself with the thought that in Germany things are not nearly so bad, I must plainly tell him, *"De te fabula narratur."*

Intrinsically, it is not a question of the higher or lower degree of development of the social antagonisms that result from the natural laws of capitalist production. It is a question of these laws themselves, of these tendencies working with iron necessity toward inevitable results. The country that is more developed industrially only shows, to the less developed, the image of its own future.

But apart from this. Where capitalist production is fully naturalized among the Germans (for instance, in the factories proper) the condition of things is much worse than in England, because the counter-poise of the Factory Acts is wanting. In all other spheres, we, like all the rest of Continental Western Europe, suffer not only from the development of capitalist production, but also from the incompleteness of that development. Alongside of modern evils, a whole series of inherited evils oppress us, arising from the passive survival of antiquated modes of production, with their inevitable train of social and political anachronisms. We suffer not only from the living but from the dead. *Le mort saisit le vif!* (*Capital,* pp. 12–13.)

The interested reader will, I hope, already have forgiven me for breaking my rule against long quotations, because of the extraordinary richness and complexity of thought of these paragraphs. Here we have a perfect example of why it is impossible to accept or reject Marx "as a whole," for we will undertake to disentangle two different lines of thought, one of which we will give reasons for rejecting, and the other we adopt as the central thesis of the present study.

It is clear that since America did not follow the pattern of "the more developed" England, or find the image of its own future there, it is this line of thought that we reject. Now the question is, whether there is not a more generalized, theoretical ground for rejection of this thought. In its most simple form, that similar conditions when worked upon by uniform laws produce similar effects, there is of course no possible objection to it, and it is one of those commonplace but necessary laws found in all branches of scientific thought. But we have already seen that in dealing with America, Marx had interpreted it in the sense that uniformity of law would with "iron necessity" produce uniform effects even when applied to dissimilar material. This is the thought that must be rejected.

We may agree with Engels that there was *necessity* at work behind the succession of different dominant powers in world economy. The fact that Flanders rose to pre-eminence in the sixteenth century was doubtless the *necessary* result of certain ascertainable factors. That Flanders declined, to be replaced by Holland, was equally the result of necessity, as well as the replacement of the Dutch by England, and the English by America. But the idea that each dominant power showed to its potential successor the "image of its own future" does not follow from this and is unacceptable. We *know* that in the case of America her future dominance became *necessary,* not from the laws of capitalism which she shared with England, but from the conditions that produced the free land system, which she did not share with England. We may assume that in each such succession of one power to pre-eminence over another there was a *necessity* arising from a *difference* in the rising power as compared with the declining one, and that this difference lay in the conditions rather than the laws.

Marx's analogy with the method of the physicist who studies phenomena in their "purest" examples obtainable may be accepted as justifying the choice of England as the "classic ground" rather than any continental European country. England was a more "pure" example of capitalism than the Continent. But England was less "pure" than America in this respect. It is true that America had not yet replaced England as world economic leader when Marx wrote *Capital,* but she was already casting such a long shadow ahead that Marx and Engels had for years been predicting her eventual supremacy. Unquestionably America in the mid-nineteenth century already presented the most reliable "norm" of the "pure" capitalist economy "free from the disturbing influences" of feudalism and other alien, pre-capitalist systems. And equally certain it is, that if Marx had taken America as his "classic ground," he could not have substantiated even approximately the subsistence-wage theory and the doctrine of impoverishment.

Finally, on the broadest lesson that can be drawn from the comparison between nations, I quote with complete agreement the words of Marx that identify the central factor in the economic progress of nations, the degree of freedom enjoyed by the producers. In the same preface quoted above Marx said:

> Apart from higher motives, therefore, their own most important interests dictate to the classes that are for the nonce the ruling ones, the removal of all legally removable hindrances to the free development of the working class. For this reason, as well as others, I have given so large a space in this volume to the history, the details, and the results of the English factory legislation. One nation can and should learn from others. (*Ibid.,* p. 14.)

V.

A MATHEMATICAL ANALYSIS OF THE SOCIAL WAGE

WE PAUSE NOW, from the direct examination of Marx's thought, in order to give precision to our thesis by a mathematical analysis of the structure of the social wage. The question posed is the relative weight of subsistence as against the social increment above subsistence in wages. We are able to come to grips with this problem by means of a comparative examination of wages a century ago and those of today.

There are many difficulties in establishing relative measurement of wages as between country and country, and even more in comparing century with century. John Strachey has made a most valuable examination of these in Chapter 6 of his *Contemporary Capitalism,* to which I would refer those who wish to study that problem in detail. His conclusion that index figures currently used for this purpose have a substantial validity, even if subject to improvements in precision, is one that is accepted by the main body of economic thought regardless of political bias. Certainly Marx and the most conservative economists of today could have found common ground on this point. And since this chapter is concerned not at all with *statistical* precision, but entirely with the definition of the order of magnitude of various factors in their relations to one another, which we have already accepted in a more general form with sources cited, and now only restate in mathematical terms, the method of index figures is a matter of course.

Subsistence is difficult, if not impossible, to define statistically. No economist has even attempted to measure empirically that minimum amount of commodities which will keep the worker at his job and enable him to reproduce himself. Yet every economist has dealt with this as an ascertainable magnitude, at least in approximation. Among the possible ways of arriving at such approximations, for example, would be to accept a modern experiment in subsistence as a standard, namely, that set by the United Nations Refugee Commission in dealing with Arab displaced persons in the Arab-Israeli dispute, which roughly measures subsistence at seven American cents per day. Or another variant might be to take a large low-wage country as the standard, if its population has grown over the centuries, thus proving that its wage level is not below subsistence, such a country as India, for example. Such hypothetical approximations of subsistence, which ignore the complications involved in the difference between degrees and levels of industrialization, open up so many possibilities of controversy that they are unsatisfactory for our purpose, which is, after all, to find some sort of valid comparison between the industrialized countries.

Looking for the least controversial of such approximations of subsistence, we may, therefore, confine ourselves to the three main areas between which we have already made comparison, and found their wage levels to be represented by the comparative figures of 1, 2, and 4 in the mid-nineteenth century, namely, the industrial lands of continental Europe,

England, and America. Here we take the continental level as subsistence, discounting the possible margin in that level above subsistence as our margin of error. The index of subsistence, therefore, is 1.00. The British wage is represented by 2.00 and the American by 4.00.

Subsistence, being a function of a definite quantity of physical commodities, is the *least variable* factor entering into wages, particularly as we are dealing with *real wages* and price fluctuations are thereby excluded. We may therefore assume that it is *constant,* admitting that here again we have introduced a margin of possible error to the degree that it can be shown that variation actually took place. Such margins of possible error do not disturb us, however, since the largest hypothetically possible error would not significantly change the *relative order of magnitude* which we are seeking.[1]

Wages consist of two unknown magnitudes, the subsistence base or floor, and the social increment above that base. Mathematical techniques provide the shortest and most precise way to define the relationship between unknown factors, though it can also be done by simple logic. We put our basic assumptions stated above into mathematical equations of a rather elementary type, in which the first term is subsistence and is constant (identified as x), the second term is the social increment and is variable (identified as y, y', and y'', for the Continent, England, and America), and the sum of the two terms is equal to the total wage.

Our assumptions stated thus as equations are as follows:

First equation: (continental wage, mid-nineteenth century)

$$x + y = 1.00$$

[1] In my lectures at Rutgers University in November 1957, which were an earlier version of the present study, I limited the comparison to England and America, and the index figure started from the English base, not the continental. The present base does not change more than details, and gives the same over-all picture.

Second equation: (English wage, mid-nineteenth century)

$$x + y' = 2.00$$

Third equation: (American wage, mid-nineteenth century)

$$x + y'' = 4.00$$

Our assumption that the continental wage is equal to subsistence, or x, informs us that y is equal to zero, that y' equals 1.00, and that y'' equals 3.00; or, in other words, the English social increment is equal to the total continental wage, and the American social increment is equal to three times the continental total wage or three times the English social increment. The ratios of social increment to subsistence can be stated for the Continent as 0:1, for England as 1:1, and for America as 3:1, for the mid-nineteenth century.

Now to carry the comparison to the mid-twentieth century we drop the continental figure, since we have no authority at hand for a reliable estimate of the continental advance in wages over the century. For the English wage, we unhesitatingly adopt the estimates of John Strachey that it doubled over the century. For the relative American wage, we compare the exact statistics of the United Nations showing comparable wages of industrial workers in America and England (a reliable indicator of the general wage differential) showing something more than a three-to-one ratio favoring America, and further confirm this by finding comparative social-security benefits in the two countries at the same ratio. Now we extend our second and third equations above stated, and obtain for mid-twentieth century the following:

Fourth equation: (English wage, mid-twentieth century)

$$x + [\, x + 2y' \,] = 4.00$$

Fifth equation: (American wage, mid-twentieth century)

$$x + [\, 2x + 3y'' \,] = 12.00$$

Thus we learn that the current English social increment is equal to three times the continental wage of a century ago;

while the American social increment is eleven times the same figure. Otherwise stated, the ratio of social increment to subsistence in the English wage is now as 3:1, and in the American wage it is as 11:1.

It is fully clear that with any even plausible margin of error in our assumptions, it would not seriously change the order of magnitude revealed in the above figures, and that we were justified in ignoring it.

In any case, we have demonstrated that the social increment above subsistence in wages is the dynamic and major factor in all the industrially advanced countries. And if we were to compare from any one of many possible different bases, we would obtain slightly varying ratios but the same over-all picture.

The "mathematical accuracy" we have thus introduced into the concept of the social wage is, of course, entirely relative to our basic assumptions; that is, we have merely given a precise definition of what those assumptions mean. The assumptions themselves rest on historical evidence, and stand or fall with that evidence.

VI.

MARX AND THE LATEST INDUSTRIAL REVOLUTION

OUR re-examination of Marx in the light of American experience in the nineteenth century has already thrown a good deal of light on the modern problems of America. Let us now see if it is not possible to focus that light more sharply, taking up first the modern problem called "automation," which has come to signify that complex of questions involved in the latest industrial revolution.

So far, I am afraid, American students of Marx have contributed but little to the study of automation, largely because they are entangled in the Marxist dogmas. The organized labor movement has approached that study pragmatically, concentrating its attention upon the readjustments that will be required when the promises of automation are realized, for the protection of labor's standards—a most praiseworthy aim, but one from which the urgency is taken away somewhat by the current recognition that *the new industrial revolution has been stalled* for some unexplained reason. America's present problem is not so much that automation is creating a new situation as that the old situation is holding back the realization of automation. It is to this neglected view of the problem that we first direct our thought.

Tremendous changes in the world have occurred since

Marx studied the revolutions accompanying the rise of modern industry in the eighteenth and nineteenth centuries. It is not the same world, and in many vital aspects Marx would not recognize our modern society as the capitalism he knew. Yet we must recognize that *in principle* automation in the most modern sense is merely a hugely multiplied copy of the earlier rise of modern machinery, which Marx defined as "a huge automaton." The modern name of "automation" could just as validly have been applied to the problems of one and two centuries ago. The name, therefore, does not express the difference between the two periods, but rather hides it. For while *in principle* the problem remains the same, its *historical setting* is very different, and its enormously expanded scale has changed the *quality* of the problem. We may compare this with the change that has taken place in war, where the advent of explosive power so great that *one bomb* can today wreak more destruction than *all previous bombs in all the wars of history combined* has quite wiped out the foundations of military science that were laid by Von Clausewitz when he defined war as "the continuation of politics by other means."

The transition from simple manufacture to modern machine industry, in the eighteenth and nineteenth centuries, involved the technology of incorporating many tools into one large automatic machine and the application of power resources to move the machine that had hitherto been unusable or even unknown. It was also much more than this technological process, in that it required a profound reorganization of the social relations among men. All the upheavals and revolutions of the eighteenth and nineteenth centuries, and down to the present, have the common character, behind all their differences, that they are efforts to reconstruct social and political relations, the institutional framework within which men work together, to create room for the development of the expanding productive forces represented in the "huge automatons" of machinery. Marx's supreme contribution to thought was that he showed that the rising technology transformed the conditions under which men lived and worked together, made possible and necessary the change of their institutions in the direction of ever more freedom, and set the historical task of abolishing poverty.

Marx's "huge automaton" of a century ago is now, in the mid-twentieth century, become the completely automatic factory, striving rapidly toward an "ideal" type in which the role of labor is confined to supervision and repair, with raw material entering at one end on a conveyor to emerge from the other end as finished product without the turning of a single human hand except upon the automatic control buttons.

While in principle Marx studied exactly the same problem, in practical life, in its historical setting, the modern problem is as different from that of Marx's day as the advent of supersonic air travel and the immediate prospect of travel in outer space differs from Fulton's first steamship and the first locomotives.

In facing the machine that Marx knew, the more primitive methods of production prevailing in simple manufacture shriveled up and died. They left behind those formerly employed in them as a "stagnant surplus population," in large part destined never again to find employment. These human victims of machinery furnished Marx with the factual base for his version of the old doctrine of impoverishment; he collected in *Capital* an impressive documentation on the wiping out through pauperism of a whole generation of artisans, whose skills had been rendered obsolete by the machine, beginning in textiles and extending to all industries.

It required the English Factory Acts and years of civil struggle to pull England out of this bog of impoverishment. This was the period when America was jumping forward ahead of England, because free land had created a shortage of population instead of a surplus, so that the rise of modern industry merely made up for the deficiency of heads and hands. This gave labor a position of power in America, which in England was gained only in prolonged struggle, and even then not to the degree of America. This power of labor is the foundation of all modern democracy, and in its absence there is no escape from the tendency of "huge automatons" to displace labor, render it redundant, and thereby pauperize it.

Democracy in the sense of an effective universal adult suffrage in potential control of national policy is an achievement of the twentieth century, and is still confined to a few of the most advanced countries. It arose as a prolonged evolutionary process in which America led the way. In the earliest days of industrialization, the struggle of the workers to escape impoverishment imposed by machinery took the form of direct struggle against the machine itself. Marx gathered in *Capital* an imposing array of records of such struggles from the sixteenth to the eighteenth centuries, and even into the nineteenth. One of these records he found in a book by Abbe Lancelotti, published in Venice in 1636, but written in 1579, and referring to events a half-century earlier, reveals how the introduction of machinery was delayed for hundreds of years. It relates that

> Anthony Müller of Danzig saw about 50 years ago in that town, a very ingenious machine, which weaves 4 to 6 pieces at once. But the Mayor being apprehensive that this invention might throw a large number of workmen on the street, caused the inventor to be secretly strangled or drowned. (*Capital,* p. 467.)

Only some two hundred years later did textile machines come into general use, long after the technological process had been discovered. Undoubtedly this prolonged delay was the result, in the main, of the fear of the population of that mass impoverishment which did, in fact, mark the first century of machinery especially in continental Europe, where the remnants of feudalism were strongest. This fear was still alive and strong in the England of Marx's time, although it was always relatively absent in America.

Wherever the despotism of capital exists in its most primitive sense, that is, where capital is able to drive down wages to subsistence levels, to that same degree there is ground for this fear of machines among the workers. For it is only in the social context of rising social influence and power on the part of labor that the benefits of machinery can be distributed widely among the workers and the general population.

Furthermore, it was only to the extent that this threat of technological unemployment was overcome that the higher levels of industrialization could be reached. While the threat of unemployment was real and active, it produced one of two results: either the resistance of the workers prevented the introduction of machinery, halting industrialization, or the machinery introduced without controls over the primitive greed of capital resulted in an impoverished population and a stunted economy. Even the law of profit rebels against mass impoverishment, and punishes it with a low rate of accumulation. Historically considered, no nation has ever been able to attain the higher levels of industrialization and productivity that are inherent in machinery unless and until it raised the general standard of living of its population in approximately an equal ratio.

Wherever wage standards have been maintained and advanced, there in the same degree has the fear of machinery and resistance to its introduction been allayed among the workers. The working people, although still by and large uninformed on the theoretical aspects of the problem, have gained through experience an instinctive wisdom, and confidence in their ability to control the possible harmful effects of machinery and higher technology in general, and thereby to share its gains. It is significant that in America, land of the highest development of machinery, there is the least fear of it among workers. Such a fear is no longer a big obstacle to technological advance in America.

Nevertheless, nothing is more obvious in America today than the fact that something is holding up the new industrial revolution involved in automation. The rhythm of the American economy, in the face of enormously enhanced possibilities of growth, has definitely been declining, and in 1958 has even shown signs of receding in the absolute sense. And the coincidence that this moment of American decline takes place when the Soviet Union makes spectacular advances symbolized in the "sputniks" has shocked America out of its complacency, and created a crisis of confidence. The unease, sometimes bordering on panic, that has gripped some high circles in America in face of these developments, is not necessarily any more promising of improvement than the smugness it replaced. Indeed, the new craze for "crash programs," "czars" to take over direction here, there, and everywhere, "emergency programs" each one more superficial than the one it replaces, all combine to point up the danger of a "crisis of the regime" quite distinct from the real economic problems facing the country, and quite unnecessary and harmful as panic is always unnecessary and harmful.

Let us test our whole review and analysis of the rise of American economy to a leading position in the world by asking what sort of approach it would suggest for meeting the current critical problems. How should we, in this light, formulate the problems, understanding that the form in which a question is put usually contains half the answer?

American scientists and engineers have solved in principle all the technological problems of building completely automated factories from raw material to finished product, wherein the necessary labor is reduced to supervision, maintenance, and repair. Model or experimental "guide plants" have with varying degrees of completeness proved the practical applicability of these principles to a wide range of economic activities, ranging from the production of all types of steel, through automobile manufactures, down to office work and accounting. The increase in productivity per labor unit involved ranges from 50 per cent upward to 300 per cent, taking into account the labor involved in producing the new plants themselves, in the first stage of their mass utilization. The American economy holds in its hands all the material and technological means to double the national production within a short term of years, and then to proceed with subsequent redoubling in ever-shortening terms. Without wasting any time in quibbles about the precise measurement of those time periods, we can sum up the expansive power of the productive forces compared with the past period as being of a similar order of magnitude as the expanded capacity of military destructive power today over that of World War II. This is the essential outline of the scope of the new industrial revolution that has matured in the heart of American society. These are the forces for expansion of American economy to a distinctively higher historical level that exist and cry out to be used.

The higher productive powers are not, however, being utilized on a mass scale, and we know their tremendous potentiality only from the laboratory and experimental samples that have proved the applicability of their principles. Our technological level has once more surpassed our social ability to use it. Our social relations and mode of organization which were crystallized at a lower technological level are proving themselves unable to make use of the higher technology in order to rise to a higher level.

What are the obstacles? They do not lie in any fear of, or hostility to, the higher technology on the part of labor. We have explained the receptivity of American labor to such progress and the historical reasons for it; labor requires only the simple safeguards and guarantees of a social distribution that retains the present ratio set under a lower level, when the higher is introduced. There is no obstacle in lack of accumulation, for one of America's sharpest problems is how to make use of idle accumulation; and we have the example that America had no serious difficulty, starting from the production level of the 1930's, in finding $360,000,000,000 to "invest" in the destruction of war, a greater sum than is involved in the complete reconstruction of our economy on the automative model, the added product of which would repay the cost in at most two or three years. There is no material obstacle. All the obstacles exist in the mode of thinking, the checks and balances, the special interests of institutions and groups, that grew up and were crystallized into decision-making power under the old and lower technology. This is the decisive problem of the new industrial revolution, and because we are not solving it, we are sliding backward into an economic recession instead of moving forward to new levels.

America responded to the sputniks and all the things they stand for with fear, and a certain degree of panic, largely because of the unsolved problems of the new industrial revolution. Certainly if America were making use of all its assets, there could be no fear of Russia in any field of competitive co-existence, but only the common fear of all the world that the wild men on either side might unleash atomic war. For America is ahead of Russia in every field except the rate of expansion, and if and when she learns to use all her assets, she will again lead Russia in that field also. If the competition of Russia shakes America out of her lethargy in this respect, that is all to the good if America responds without panic, and with a realistic facing of the necessities of the new industrial revolution.

Of course if America continues to falter in rate of growth, and even slides into a depression, then there is no real contest with Russia who thus wins by default. As an extreme example of how this works, we may take a look at Khrushchev's boast that Russia will soon be producing more food than America. The Russians can hardly lose this competition, except in the unlikely case of their inner collapse, because they are exerting great efforts to expand agricultural production while the American government is spending billions to reduce it. It is true that America reduces production with great difficulty, even as Russia expands with great difficulty, but no matter how difficult each side finds its task, government policy on each side is working toward the goal of Khrushchev's boast, and will probably succeed. America is not oriented toward growth, so far as governmental policy is concerned, and what growth takes place occurs despite that policy.

There was a curious moment at the Twentieth Congress of the Russian Communist party in 1956, which illustrates some of the complexity of the problem. The leader Mikoyan told the delegates that in America the government pays billions of dollars to remove land from cultivation, while in Russia vast new lands are being opened up. The report in

Pravda noted laconically, in parentheses, that there was "commotion in the hall." One can only imagine the mixed motives of that commotion. The clear implication that America is a land of idiots may also have aroused other emotions, such as amazement at such riches that could afford that degree of idiocy, and suspicion that America could not, as they had been told, have stolen all those riches from the rest of the world. How can the Russians understand that in the American social context it is not idiocy but "common sense"? But when deliberate retardation and reduction of economic growth become the "common sense" of a society, that is the sure sign that the productive level has outgrown the social relationships and institutions, and unless the latter are changed there is serious trouble ahead. For the alternative to growth is not stability and the *status quo,* it is decadence and crisis. America is comparatively rich at this time, but is poor in comparison with what she can be if the vast potential productive powers are put to use, for we could double the national production in a fraction of a decade. Our choice is between becoming much richer or becoming much poorer, for it is impossible to freeze the *status quo*. We can go forward or backward, but we cannot stand still.

America's current top-flight decision makers seem to be hypnotized by the *status quo* as the only possible answer to all questions, although all history is witness that it is the most impossible of all answers. As they reveal their thoughts in public discussions, they seem to say that to hold fast to the *status quo* is the only alternative to copying the Soviet way of advance through an authoritarian, semi-militarist dictatorship, the abandonment of the free and democratic development in which America pioneered. This curious capitulation to the dogmas of Russian communism, which we witness taking place in the minds of the spokesmen of the cold war against that same Russian communism, is one of the little ironies of history. For it takes place at a moment when the Russian leaders, while insisting upon these dogmas among their followers, have discarded them completely in their own thinking, and have become the world's most consistent pragmatists and opportunists.

It is by no means certain that Russian technological advance is *because of or despite* the authoritarian nature of the Soviet regime. I would say it is despite the dictatorship, but the subject is beyond our scope in the present discussion, which deals primarily with America. And certainly for America, the whole idea of authoritarian development of the new industrial revolution, in any form, is almost as fantastically unreal as the idea of standing still and going neither forward nor back. But it is a tribute to the power of Russian propaganda, if not to the intellectual stature of current American statesmen, to hear the latter say that this country cannot match Russian achievements because we cannot copy their political methods—and this at a moment when even the American communist party has dissolved down to a handful of fanatics because of disillusionment with those Russian political methods!

The historical evidence indicates that the new industrial revolution, like its predecessor of the eighteenth and nineteenth centuries, must find its realization through expanding, not contracting, the area of freedom and democratic self-government. If there are any apparent exceptions to this rule, certainly they are not to be found in the historical and material situation of America. Above all America has nothing to copy from the political and social methods of the Soviet Union, because that would mean going backward. We have already achieved a higher level than they, and our own experience shows that we achieved it through expanding democracy. The problems of the new industrial revolution indicate a similar way forward today.

The new industrial revolution will call for, on an ever-growing scale, new sources of raw material and foods, and new forms of power, more and more the synthetic products of technology as contrasted with the "natural" forms of the previous era. Such a technological society calls for a radical deepening and spread of technical skills and general education throughout the population, together with general, consciously held social ideals and purposes—what might be called a social faith if we exclude from that concept all dogmas and doctrines, which are intrinsically divisive—as the basis for individual behavior and the decisions of central institutions. These things cannot be produced by authority, they cannot be spread by indoctrination, and governments can help create them usually only by creating conditions known to be favorable to their growth. The direct role of government in these long-range and basic requirements is not primary and authoritarian, but secondary and in the provision of social means.

In the immediate measures necessary to open the way to the new industrial revolution, the role of government is more direct, although by no means to be permitted to limit freedoms. Only through governmental action, to take a main example, is it possible to divert a growing part of the national surplus from its thoroughly wasteful use for military purposes, to its proper use to expand productivity both here and abroad. Only through governmental actions is it possible to free the scientific community from its bondage to the military services, and release its tremendous potential for the enrichment of civil life in all ways, including production. Only by governmental action can the expansion of scientific and technological personnel on the required scale be secured, by scholarships on a scale broad enough to absorb all the most promising youth, and administered by the scientific community itself to guarantee the best results.

Now to come a step closer to the direct stimulation of the new industrial revolution, there is the means of the declaration of public policy by the government (congressional, administrative, or both) demanding of all industry in the national interest the speediest possible adoption of the higher and more productive technology, the mobilization of public support for this demand through investigations, reports, and discussions, and the setting up of institutes to study and report on progress being made. It is of course understood that such policy and study cover the problem of full utilization of existing productive forces, maintenance of full employment, and the problem of markets for the expected expansion of national product.

The final step of governmental intervention in the productive process itself may or may not become necessary. In principle it cannot be excluded from the prospect, for that would be to invite the sabotage of special interests profiting from the limitation of production. In practice, it should be the last resort, when and where the measures of education and pressure have failed to secure the expected and possible results.

All of the foregoing is not a program or platform, but merely a series of suggestions to show how a free and democratic society is not helpless when its economic system begins to hesitate and stall, that it is not at the mercy of the automatic working of the system, that "revolutionary" removal of obstacles to progress need not be wholesale overturns, but may be discriminating remedies for precisely defined difficulties.

The doctrinaires of both Right and Left will consider this

whole approach to modern problems as unrealistic and "utopian." In this they will be echoing, some consciously and others unconsciously, the dogma of Moscow that capitalism in general, and the American example in particular, is doomed by its inner contradictions to a wholesale and revolutionary downfall, that will leave only ruins upon which socialism will be built. My own education by Marx and others, after removing the Marxian dogmas, teaches me otherwise, that while all progress comes through the working out of such inner contradictions, this may be accomplished peacefully and without catastrophes if and where the level of social intelligence has reached a certain height, and where the productive forces are strong and hold the immediate promise of general social well-being for all. As Marx put it:

"... Mankind always sets itself only such tasks as it can solve ...; the task itself only arises when the material conditions for its solution already exist."

VII.

"ABSOLUTE AND RELATIVE IMPOVERISHMENT"

THE ancient doctrine of impoverishment, which Marx incorporated into his scientific analysis of capitalism to its detriment, has been given its most modern dress by the Russian neo-dogmatists under the name of "the law of absolute and relative impoverishment."

While it is put forward in the name of Marx, it could, with more accuracy, be named after a more ancient writer, the monk and economist, G. Ortes, who wrote, *in 1777,* that

> In the economy of a nation ... the abundance of wealth with some people, is always equal to the want of it with others; the great riches of a small number are always accompanied by the absolute privation of the first necessities of life for many others. The wealth of a nation corresponds with its population, and its misery corresponds with its wealth.

With the Russians "the law" is very vague and undefined, but has been called into operation with deadly effects on individual economists who were accused of neglecting it in their writings. Thus, for example, the economist Eugene Varga, after well over a quarter-century career as a leading scientific figure in Moscow, Director of the Institute of World Economics under the Institute of Economics of the Academy of Sciences, and editor of its journal, was brought to trial for heresy before the Academy in 1947, in which one of the main charges against him was neglect of "the law of absolute and relative impoverishment." He was found guilty and banished in disgrace. This fact is sufficient to establish that "the law" is a serious business for all thinkers in the Moscow-influenced sector of the world, and thereby demands our attention.

That the new Russian version of the doctrine is something different from Marx, at least in the sense of being additional, is attested by the name they give it, which is not out of Marx. There is no mention in Marx of such categories as "absolute and relative impoverishment," and indeed it is difficult to imagine that master of logic and dialectics becoming enmeshed in such undefinable terms. It is true he used the terms "absolute and relative" with great freedom, and as categories of *surplus value* he devoted twelve chapters and some four hundred pages of *Capital* to defining and analyzing these concepts *in extenso*. But he never thought of giving even a paragraph to "absolute and relative impoverishment." The only thing that impoverishment can be made "relative" to is the subsistence level, below which it begins, and presumably once it appears it is "absolute," at least in the sense of being *real,* though any other possible sense seems quite vague and mysterious.

The "law of absolute and relative impoverishment" remains undefined in Russian economic textbooks. Thus the treatise chosen in 1946 for translation into many languages, by the well-known economist A. Leontiev (an American edition appearing as *Marx's Capital,* International Publishers, New York, 1946), has only one sentence on it, reading:

"Only Marx was able to demonstrate the inevitability of the absolute and relative impoverishment of the proletariat under capitalism as a law. . . ."

This only passes the buck back to Marx, without even a token attempt to explain how Marx could "demonstrate" an absolute and relative law he never mentioned in *Capital.* Perhaps Leontiev's claim that "only Marx" could do this was a subtle way of washing his own hands of a disagreeable business, where he was constrained by orthodoxy to repeat a phrase that was senseless.

Examining some of the postwar citations of the "law" in the Russian theoretical organ, *Bolshevik,* we gain little more insight into its nature. Thus, in No. 17, September 15, 1947, reporting the "guilty of heresy" verdict against Varga, M. Gladkov explains that among Varga's sins or crimes, in his book *Changes in the Economy of Capitalism,* was the fact that:

> Instead of demonstrating the absolute and relative pauperization of the proletariat, Varga confines himself to an abstract assertion that "pauperization . . . theoretically is occurring constantly."

But if that was a sin on Varga's part, it was one he shared with the entire Moscow Institute, since the two-day trial of Varga discloses in its record not a single book being cited as doing what Varga was accused of neglecting. They all merely did what they accused Varga of, gave "abstract assertions" of the law and dipped their fingers in the holy water. And in all the years since then I have not heard of any book appearing from the Institute "demonstrating" the "law of absolute and relative impoverishment." Varga was just as "orthodox" as the rest of them who tried him and found him guilty of heresy.

Another example may be found in No. 23, December 15, 1948, where the economist I. Kuzminov publishes an article entitled "Concerning the Crisis-Character of Economic Development in the United States After the War." Here Kuzminov argues that it is a mistake to say there was an economic boom in America after the war, that, on the contrary, there was a constantly deepening economic crisis, and that to speak of factors making for an economic boom such as "postponed demand" would be in "evident contradiction to the law of absolute and relative impoverishment." Kuzminov would have been correct if he had said that the existence of American capitalism was itself in "evident contradiction to the law of impoverishment in general." But since Marx's analysis of the laws of motion of capitalist production, including the impoverishment doctrine, had as its outstanding feature the concept of "the cycle" of boom and bust so long as capitalism existed, it is clear that Kuzminov was not basing himself on Marx's original doctrine, but upon a new Russian version.

This undefined and mysterious law has been erected into a decisive test of "orthodoxy," so powerful that on charges of neglecting it whole institutes are abolished, journals suppressed, and long-honored names are dragged in the mud. We have been looking for some *rational* explanation of this "law" and its use to establish a reign of intellectual terror among Soviet economists and those abroad who follow them.

Our inability to find any *rational* basis for the "law" or the way it has been utilized in public discussion suggests that we must find its reason for being *in its arbitrariness, lack of rational basis, and vagueness.*

From this approach the new dogma appears as one of the classical devices for thought control. It gathers around itself the age-old sanctity of the doctrine of impoverishment. It claims the dignity of "law" but avoids any precise definition. It calls the authority of Marx to its aid but separates itself from Marx's text by a new name, to avoid being pinned down to any definite standard. It discards everything that could make it predictable and rational, for its purpose is terrorization, and the rational disperses terror. The instrument of terror must be unpredictable, its blows must hit the blameworthy and the blameless indiscriminately, so that every man will say to himself, "I may be next." It must be known only by the blows it delivers, and these must be unpredictable. In this light we are no longer puzzled by the fact that Varga, far from being an innovator of new economic thought, was one of the most orthodox of Soviet economists. In his very blamelessness and mediocrity lay the chief reason he was chosen as victim; if Varga could be struck down as a heretic, then it could literally happen to anyone without warning.

The "beauty" of such an undefined "law," as an instrument of intellectual terror, lies in the fact that since no one knows just what it is no one can refute it. Thus it is an ideal instrument of rule for an impersonal bureaucracy. It is the glorification of irrationality, it is the liquidation of all law. We will therefore abandon any further search for any connection of the "law" with Marx's thought, for Marx even in his mistakes was the very embodiment of rationality, and he himself gave us the instruments for correcting them.

That does not mean there is no historical background to the phrase "absolute and relative impoverishment." It is very interesting to glance for a moment at that background.

Marx and Engels, in the years following the publication of *Capital,* were forced to note that English wages continued to rise rather than decline to subsistence, and that American wages continued more than twice the English level. Their own reactions to this fact we will, in the main, examine in the next chapter in connection with a larger issue. Here it is sufficient to note that they always, in the end, confirmed the inevitability of impoverishment in every capitalist country, to be escaped *only* by the socialist revolution. Thus Engels wrote to Florence Wischnewetsky, February 3, 1886, that:

"... Even in America the condition of the working class must gradually sink lower and lower." (*Selected Correspondence,* p. 443.)

After the death of Marx and Engels, the Marxist party met and defeated the "revisionism" of the Bernstein school, at the cost, however, of a certain revisionism of their own on the impoverishment issue. It became permissible, not to reject the impoverishment doctrine, but to "interpret" it in the sense that it would not necessarily be realized as actual impoverishment until the final crisis of capitalism, but that it was revealed as a permanent tendency of capitalism, at all times, in the decline of the share of the worker in the total product, "relative" to the share of the capitalist.

With the outbreak of World War I, however, the revolutionary wing of Marxism, headed by Lenin, which was more boldly revisionist in its own way than the Kautsky wing, but formally more dogmatic, declared that now the time had passed forever when the workers could make economic gains as a class. The earliest precise definition of this judgment of a new period that I have found was written in 1915 by N. Bukharin, in his book *Imperialism and World Economy,* for which Lenin wrote an approving introduction. On page 159 Bukharin wrote:

A deep-going tendency towards decreasing real wages must be noted first of all.... An ever greater part of the national product will be retained by the bourgeoisie and its state.... Workers' gain that were a usual phenomenon in the former epoch become almost impossible. There takes place, not a relative, but also an *absolute* worsening of the situation of the working class.

This is probably the origin of *the phrase* "absolute and relative" impoverishment. "Relative impoverishment," which had appeared in the previous period as a means of holding on to the impoverishment doctrine in the face of rising wage levels, was here, probably for the first time, coupled with "absolute" impoverishment, the meaning being simply that real wages were actually going to decline, not merely in ratio to the national product. I have emphasized that this is probably the historical origin of *the phrase,* whose formulation was not an analysis of two categories of "absolute and relative impoverishment," but merely the accidental form of stating the judgment that a period when the impoverishment doctrine did not operate, in the industrially advanced lands, had come to an end, and the original Marx doctrine was to be reinstated in full force. The Russian neo-dogmatists after World War II have used the phrase in their new form, "the law of absolute and relative impoverishment," in quite a different context, indicated by their stubborn evasion of any historical or textual definition of their "law." The last thing they would accept publicly is its origin in Bukharin's book, not only because Bukharin is one of those they have erased from history, but even more because Bukharin recognized that there had been a long period when rising real wage levels "were a usual phenomenon."

What happens to the ideology of simple followers of Marxism, when faced with the new "law of absolute and relative impoverishment," is another question. Inevitably they try to understand the "law" as something rational, dealing with two types of impoverishment, but with equal inevitability they fall into much confusion in the process.

The most vulgar or "popular" form of understanding says very simply that poverty must be conceived broadly as a relative matter, that one is in poverty "relative" to others who have greater access to worldly goods. Thus the only unimpoverished man is he than whom no other can be said to have more. The millionaire who says: "I am too poor to maintain two yachts," and the common laborer who says: "I am too poor to have two shirts," are both, and with equal justification, pleading relative impoverishment, although "absolute impoverishment" is true only of the latter. One worthy scholar who explained this to me became personally insulted when I suggested this was the doctrine expounded by the comic-strip "Keeping Up with the Joneses." He said I should not turn serious questions into a joke, and could not see that his theory made a joke of economics itself.

A more sophisticated rationalization of "the law" refers itself accurately to a quotation from Marx, which says: "While real wages may rise, they can never rise proportionately to the productive powers of labor." That proposition was one of Marx's mistakes, but even if taken as correct it relates only to the ratio of distribution of the product between capital and labor, and not to impoverishment. Impoverishment, no matter how it may be qualified, enters into the economic picture *at that point where living standards fall below the subsistence level.* The ratio of distribution, important in its own right as a separate question, has nothing to do with the determination of when or where pauperism becomes a fact. The mixing up of these different questions, in the minds of the hapless student trying to rationalize "the law of absolute and relative impoverishment," ends precise thinking and throws all categories into one undifferentiated lump of sour dough.

Marx made it clear when formulating the "absolute general law" of impoverishment that he was referring to the unemployed and the unemployable workers—as he said, the "lazarus-layer," "whose misery is in inverse ratio to its torments of labor," and for whom state aid meant only the untold horrors of the poorhouse. The impoverished thus were primarily those who had been removed, temporarily or permanently, from the ranks of the producers, and for whom the question of a "share" in the product became a hollow mockery, since if they got everything they produced they got nothing.

The simple-minded view that the worker prospers if and when he gets a rising "share" of the product, and that he suffers when and if he gets a smaller "share," falls to pieces the moment we begin to examine the historical movement of the product to be "shared," whether it is expanding or contracting. A larger share of a rapidly declining product spells disaster to the worker, while a smaller "share" of a rapidly rising product spells prosperity and well-being. This was most dramatically demonstrated in the historical fact that the period of most rapid rise in the "share" of labor in the national product, in all American history, was precisely the five-year period, 1929–33, the one period since the rise of modern capitalism when pauperism became a general national problem, even if but temporarily.

If we construct a graph of the past century, on which one line represents the shifting ratio of distribution to labor of the national product, and another line represents the course of living standards of labor, the comparison would be most interesting. We would find that when the line of living standards was going up, the ratio of distribution to labor would probably, though not always, be going down; even on the rare occasions the ratio also went up it would be but slightly. And conversely, in those periods when the living standards went down, the ratio of distribution to labor showed its most marked rises. The two lines would practically never run parallel, and usually would move in opposite directions. Both lines would zigzag, but the net result over the century would be a rise of living standards of about 300 per cent, while the shifts in the ratio of distribution would cancel themselves out.

Now if we construct a similar graph comparing living standards with the course of production, then we would find, on the contrary, that the two lines tend generally to move in the same direction, when production goes up so do living standards, and on the average in the same proportion.

All the essential features of this process were analyzed in detail by Marx. If in his dogmatic conclusions he gave greater weight to the doctrine of impoverishment than to his own scientific analyses, with Marx this is strictly a rational problem, and he himself furnished us with the means to free ourselves from the dogma. But in dealing with the Russian neo-dogmatism of "the law of absolute and relative impoverishment" we are dealing with mystification and irrationality.

It was only in the course of the nineteenth century, and in the main after Marx had completed his studies, that national economic statistics became general in the countries of modern industry. Marx worked, therefore, without the wealth of statistical information which is at the command of modern economists. We must hope that some twentieth-century genius of the stature of Marx will eventually appear, to seize and remake the vast materials at our disposal, as Marx reworked the dusty archives of the British Museum. From the self-appointed "heirs of Marx" now ruling in Moscow we have learned the hard and bitter lesson to expect nothing of the kind, but only a hardening dogmatism which finally, as in the "law of absolute and relative impoverishment," extinguishes theory entirely.

In Poland, Hungary, and Yugoslavia, on the other hand, we witness the stirring again of creative Marxist thought against the paralysis of Russian dogmatism. In Italy and France there are some signs of an awakening. And in England, the work of John Strachey in the re-examination of the thought of Marx has contributed significantly to help break the bonds of dogmatism, although I disagree with his suggestion that the labor theory of value furnishes some of the roots of dogmatism.

Strachey most competently marshaled the statistical refutation of the Marxist dogma that wages can never rise in proportion to production, which is the stronghold of those who try to rationalize "relative impoverishment." His conclusion (*Contemporary Capitalism,* p. 175) is quite sound in saying

> Over the whole of the last 100 years there was, then, in Britain no "relative immiseration." (American figures were broadly similar.) Not only did the workers' standard of life more than double, but their share in the national income did not decline.

A recent American study of distribution by Gabriel Kolko (quarterly *Dissent,* winter 1957) also tends to bear out Strachey's conclusion, disclosing only very slight fluctuations in the ratio of distribution.

Even, however, if the evidence should show that the ratio of distribution to labor had declined over the century, this would not in any way change the fact that in all industrialized countries the margin above subsistence in wages grows ever wider, and that pauperism afflicts ever fewer people in those countries.

It would take too much time to follow through all the attempts to rationalize the irrational "law of absolute and relative impoverishment." Such an attempt would be as pointless as to refute, one by one, all the schemes to produce perpetual motion. Especially as those who stand as the main sponsors of "the law" before the world do not themselves find it necessary to define their law or explain how they see it at work, but only use it to turn their followers away from critical thought, we may close the present examination of the question, which may be reopened if and when the Soviet Academy of Sciences finally gets around to publishing a statement of the law and how they see it at work—something that has not been done up to the present time.[1]

[1] There is evidence in the organ of the Institute of Economics, *Voprosi Ekonomiki* (Questions of Economics), No. 11, 1957, both that the state of intellectual paralysis here described is becoming intolerable to Russian scholars and, at the same time, that they are still unable to break out of it. This journal carries a report of a discussion held on proposed revisions of the standard Russian textbook on political economy, among which is reported to be a definition of "absolute impoverishment" according to which it "may accompany a rise in real wages." Thus the necessity to recognize the obvious fact of rising real wages is acknowledged, but at the same time is cut to fit the Procrustus bed of dogma.

VIII.

DO NATIONS GROW RICH BY LOOTING OTHERS?

IT IS NOW time to face squarely the issue raised in our first chapter, the doctrine that the poverty of many nations is the source of the enrichment of a few nations, in the first place the United States of America. We have already noted that Marx and Engels never placed America in the role of looter of poorer nations, that they found the sources of her prosperity in the free relations of producers within the nation, and that they considered it in general disastrous for a nation when it subjugates another nation. This does not, however, exhaust the question, even when it is considered only in relation to the thought of Marx. Although both Marx and Engels clearly excluded America from any role of looting other nations as a source of enrichment, they did not close and lock the door against such a role for England, first because England had notoriously looted India and similar countries, second because Engels expressed the judgment that this had enriched the English economy to such an extent that even the working class had shared in the loot in the form of higher wages. If that was a sound judgment, then in principle the possibility existed that the United States might have succeeded to that role in later times.

The modern form of the doctrine of *world impoverishment*

as the opposite pole of *enrichment* of a few imperialist powers, and in the first place America, was formulated by V. I. Lenin, in his book *Imperialism, the Highest Stage of Capitalism.* Lenin made only the most formal claim to derive this doctrine from Marx directly, and that in a two-line quotation on banks as a form of universal bookkeeping. But he depended more substantially on Engels, from whom he draws two key quotations, both from private letters published only after his death, which said that the English working class was wedded to its bourgeoisie and lacked independence because of higher wages and improved living standards granted to it out of the super profits derived from the colonies and Britain's world monopolistic position. Lenin's main source for the doctrine, however, aside from his own direct contribution, was the non-Marxist English economist J. A. Hobson and the Austro-Marxist Rudolf Hilferding. It is frankly acknowledged by Leninist scholars that little if any support is to be found for the doctrine in the work of Marx and Engels published during their lifetime, and this is explained by saying: "Neither Marx nor Engels lived to see flourishing imperialism. They merely witnessed its first steps, principally in England." (Explanatory notes to Lenin, *Selected Works,* Vol. 5, p. 315.)

Marx's whole study of the rise of capitalism, and especially its most modern form, is of course pertinent to the disintegration of the primitive economies in the colonies and semi-colonial lands, under the shattering impact of commodities from the industrialized West. To cite a typical example, the textiles of Manchester not only destroyed the ancient artisan textile industry of India whose finest products had been in high demand throughout Europe during the Middle Ages; it also thereby disrupted the whole pre-capitalist economy, throwing it into an unstable revolutionary situation. The intrusion of British governmental power, in alliance with ancient ruling classes which had thus lost their bases, served to prolong the crisis and delay its resolution. All this was symbolized in the curious fact that the independence movement headed by Gandhi, the goal of which was to modernize India, took as its symbol and banner the ancient spinning wheel, although every intelligent person knew that hand spinning was as dead as the proverbial dodo bird. On all this phase of the colonial problem, Marx's work as a whole is pertinent not to say necessary to any deep understanding.

But this is not the essential issue of the doctrine of world polarization of nations into rich and poor, according to Lenin, which says the disruption of India was only the obverse side to the enrichment of England, that what one lost the other gained, that the English profit was the measure of the Indian loss, and vice-versa. On this specific issue Marx was silent,[1] and Engels gave it support in private correspondence, indirectly, by his theory that explained the workers' lack of independence by their share in the loot of imperialism.

The Leninist doctrine was saved for a long period from any penetrating criticism by the fact that all critics tended to minimize the destructive impact of the West upon the more ancient economies, and to apologize for or defend Western colonial rule of the underdeveloped countries. Since the destructive effects of both these things upon the subject countries became more and more obvious and inescapable (es-

1 Marx consistently emphasized, however, the role of subjugation of another nation as a factor holding back the whole development of the conquering nation. Ireland, as the weapon of English reaction, was his classic example. Engels wrote: "... Not only does England's internal social development remain crippled by her present relation with Ireland; her foreign policy... suffers the same fate." (Marx, *Selected Works,* Vol. 2, p. 644.) Marx said: "Ireland is therefore the great means by which the English aristocracy maintains its domination in England itself." (*Ibid.,* p. 645.) And India is spoken of as *"the Ireland of the East."* (*Ibid.,* p. 650.)

pecially to the subject peoples themselves), and the Leninist doctrine was criticized only upon these points where it was sound, its influence spread to all thinking strata in the underdeveloped lands, and to the European labor and socialist movement as well.

There is only one ground from which the Leninist dogma of world impoverishment can be attacked effectively, that is the full and unconditional recognition that the colonial system as a whole was profoundly harmful and destructive to the national life and economic development of the subjugated nations—but also that it *was equally harmful and destructive to the dominant nations*. That is to say, the vulnerable side of Lenin's dogma is the assumption that the master nations strengthened their economies and grew rich out of the booty from the colonies. Only when one grasps fully the principle that it is a disaster for any nation when it subjugates another, as damaging as that of being subjugated, is it possible successfully to refute the Leninist dogma.

It will deepen our historical perspective to recall that the "classical" colonial system, the British, was a product of the mercantilist phase of English development, and not the phase of modern industry. The industrialists were at most lukewarm in their acceptance of "empire" and, indeed, Benjamin Disraeli (Lord Beaconsfield), who rebuilt the Conservative party to include aristocrats, industrialists, and a labor and popular following on the basis of reforms, was at the same time the man who said *"the colonies are millstones around our necks"*—which did not prevent him as prime minister from later engineering the "promotion" of Queen Victoria to the title "Empress of India." Certainly the industrialists, at least, for long had no illusions that income from the colonies added strength to modern industrial development, even when they supported "the empire" for other reasons, mostly to maintain ruling coalitions with other elements. Toward the end of the nineteenth century the imperial illusion grew on the basis of expanding productivity at home, the mysterious origin of which was attributed to "the Empire," and all classes seemed to share the illusion.

A period of general expansion of industry under the impulse of the Factory Acts, Ten-Hours Bill, etc., after 1848, had resulted in the steady and general rise in the wage level. It was the result of this development that was reflected by Engels when, in a letter to Marx of October 7, 1858, he wrote the first paragraph that Lenin was to seize upon as the seal of legitimate Marxism for his doctrine of world impoverishment. Engels wrote:

> ... The English proletariat is becoming more and more bourgeois, so that this most bourgeois of all nations is apparently aiming ultimately at the possession of a bourgeois aristocracy and a bourgeois proletariat *as well as* a bourgeoisie. For a nation which exploits the whole world this is of course to a certain extent justifiable. The only thing that would help there would be a few thoroughly bad years, and since the gold discoveries these no longer seem so easy to come by. (*Selected Correspondence,* p. 116.)

In the ensuing quarter-century the prestige of "Empire" as the source of prosperity continued to mount, and Engels reflected it faithfully, even though in his own particular form, when he wrote to Karl Kautsky, September 12, 1882, the second passage which Lenin quoted to authenticate his new dogma. Engels wrote:

> You ask me what the English workers think about colonial policy. Well, exactly the same as they think about politics in general; the same as what the bourgeois think. There is no workers' party here, there are only Conservatives and Liberal-Radicals, and the workers gaily share the feast of England's monopoly of the world market and the colonies. (*Ibid.,* p. 399.)

This is not Engels at his best as thinker. I must confess that as one who rates Engels only a stage below Marx as the two greatest thinkers of the nineteenth century I wince at the spectacle of his lamentations about the incapacity of the British workers in the same sentence in which he accepts as valid the same illusion to which they had fallen victim—the illusion that there was a "feast" going on provided by monopoly and Empire, a feast that the "workers gaily share." Most of the first volume of *Capital,* and especially Marx's 1865 report (*Value, Price and Profit*), furnishes the strongest reasons to believe that it was domestic reforms and the stimulus they gave to productivity that provided what "feast" there was, and not colonial or monopoly profits. The "feast" itself, compared to modern standards, was meager. But Engels did not attack the illusion, he accepted it as valid, and only reproved the workers for being attracted to a "feast" they had won by their own struggles, but which Engels (in common with all public opinion) considered crumbs from the table of Empire.

But even Engels, under this influence, did not extend the concept to include America, but specifically limited it to England. A few years later he explained this in a letter to Florence K. Wischnewetsky in America, on February 3, 1886, in which Engels said:

> America will smash up England's industrial monopoly—whatever is left of it—but America cannot herself succeed to that monopoly. And unless *one* country has the monopoly of the markets of the world, at least in the decisive branches of trade, the conditions—relatively favorable—which existed here in England from 1848 to 1870 cannot anywhere be reproduced.... (*Selected Correspondence,* p. 443.)

Engels was wrong here in judging that the prosperity of England could nowhere be reproduced—it was far exceeded—but he was in error because he had misjudged its source as being in colonial and monopoly profits. But his judgment that America could never succeed to the British monopolist position in the world markets was accurate and sound, and, as it proved, this was an element of good fortune to the American economy.

Engels is thus seen to have given support in principle to the Leninist thesis as applied to England, but to have denied its applicability to America. For the Leninist doctrine posits America as the greatest recipient of imperialist super profits, and pictures the modern "classic" stage as being marked by many rival imperialist powers in struggle for redivision of the world, instead of *one* monopolist country, which was the *only* form in which Engels could conceive of such super profits.

We have made it clear, especially in the earlier chapters, that we give quite a different explanation than Engels to the "relatively favorable" conditions of England from 1848 onward. It is not to be found in "monopoly of the markets of the world," because it was precisely in this period that England was rapidly losing that monopoly and was facing successful American competition even within England itself—and was saved from even fiercer competition only by the fact that America's rapidly expanding domestic market kept a step ahead of her industrial expansion and diverted her products away from the export trade. It was not to be found in the colonial system, because America without colonies was enjoying even more favorable conditions, and stood twice as high in general welfare and wages. *In the very competition of America,* and her example of *high wages,* was an additional force to the reform movement in England, and thereby helped release her *inner forces* that brought about relative prosperity. That prosperity was influenced by the colonial system only as a drag and hindrance. The higher wage level in England came not from colonial super profits but from the increased productivity of English labor. Engels had been blinded to this by the dogmas of impoverishment and the subsistence wage.

In a brief theoretical analysis such as the present one it is impossible to marshal statistics in support of the argument, although in the broader picture it is important that such auxiliary work should be done. Therefore I am glad to note that John Strachey has said he will produce such a study, in that most valuable series he began with his book *Contemporary Capitalism.* He has already indicated that preliminary surveys show that "even on the basis of figures given by the most extreme exponents" of the Leninist thesis, such super profits "are simply not of the order of magnitude to sustain the argument" that they explain higher wages.

Permit me to emphasize that my own thesis goes considerably further than Strachey's on this point, inasmuch as I maintain that modern capitalism has been continuously held back in its development by the colonial system which is pre-capitalist in character. I therefore disagree with Strachey's admission that "it is undoubtedly true that colonial possessions, and imperialism generally, have greatly helped the leading capitalisms." However much they helped *capitalists* do certain things, they did not help modern capitalist industry to expand. In terms of basic economic theory, I consider Strachey's admission *equally unsound* as would be the analogous proposition that slavery in the southern United States greatly helped the development of American capitalism, because some northern capitalists shared in its profits. *Whatever* volume of profits from slavery could be shown as going to the industrial North, the fact would remain unimpaired in any degree that *slavery was the most serious impediment to industrial expansion* of the country from the days of independence to the Civil War. This I would maintain quite independently of the separate questions of political expediency involved in choosing time and method of removing the obstacle. The same considerations apply in judging the relations of English economy to the colonial empire.

This position arises not from statistics but from economic theory, the same theory Marx was expressing when he said: "How disastrous it is for a nation when it has subjugated another nation." If the theory is sound, it will find support in statistics, but statistics alone can never give birth to the theory. India as a colony was always disastrous for modern England, for its economic growth and for its wage level, just as British rule was always a disaster for India. The theory holds good despite all counter-considerations that can be adduced of incidental benefits accruing both ways.

Lenin had to strain hard to connect up his dogma of world impoverishment as the secret strength of modern capitalism, with the body of Marx's thought, by way of the private correspondence of Engels. But strain as much as he would, he could not find a direct quotation from Marx himself to sustain the dogma. In fact, his chief source for the theory was in the writings of the non-Marxist J. A. Hobson, particularly his book *Imperialism,* published in 1902. Hobson was a pacifist anti-imperialist who tried to shock the British public out of its infatuation with colonialism by picturing its "logical conclusion" in an entirely parasitic state. He followed much the same method that guided Jack London when, in the medium of the novel, *The Iron Heel*, the latter warned of the dangers in rising corporate capitalism in America. Both examples are quite legitimate propaganda, as caricatures and not as pictures of reality, not scientific works, and both become quite misleading when taken as pictures of reality. If Lenin's book *Imperialism, the Highest Stage of Capitalism,* is taken as tendentious propaganda, like *The Iron Heel,* it is also similarly legitimate; but unfortunately it was transformed into a sort of "holy book" of revealed truth, absolute truth, supposed to give the picture of the real world of capitalism above and beyond any evidence, and as ending all inquiry into the matter. In this role of a semi-religious guide to the peoples of the underdeveloped lands, and to the world communist movement, the book has become one of the greatest ideological obstacles to world understanding and world peace.

To illustrate this I will give two quotations from Hobson used by Lenin, a short one and another quite extended. He wrote:

> There is first the habit of economic parasitism, by which the ruling state has used its provinces, colonies and dependencies, in order to enrich its ruling class and to bribe its lower classes into acquiescence. (*Selected Works of V. I. Lenin,* Vol. 5, International Publishers, New York, p. 94.)

This is perhaps an adequate one-sentence description of the economic policy of the Roman Empire but becomes a caricature when applied to modern industrial countries. And while caricatures are weapons of political struggle, there are grave dangers when the political struggle is itself turned into a caricature. This is what happened when Hobson's caricature was turned by Lenin into a dogma, and by Lenin's successors into a semi-religious creed. But let us continue to quote Hobson who was appraising the economic prospects that might flow from the partition of China among the great powers, which was a subject of discussion around the turn of the century. Hobson says:

> The greater part of Western Europe might then assume the appearance and character already exhibited by tracts of country in the South of England, in the Riviera, and in the tourist-ridden

and residential parts of Italy and Switzerland, little clusters of wealthy aristocrats drawing dividends and pensions from the Far East, with a somewhat larger group of professional retainers and tradesmen and a large body of personal servants and workers in the transport trade and in the final stages of production of the more perishable goods; all the main arterial industries would have disappeared, the staple foods and manufactures flowing in as tribute from Asia and Africa.

We have foreshadowed the possibility of even a larger alliance of Western states, a European federation of great powers which, so far from forwarding the cause of world civilization, might introduce the gigantic peril of a Western parasitism, a group of advanced industrial nations, whose upper classes draw vast tribute from Asia and Africa, with which they support great tame masses of retainers, no longer engaged in the staple industries of agriculture and manufacture, but kept in the performance of personal or minor industrial services under the control of a new financial aristocracy. Let those who would scout such a theory as undeserving of consideration examine the economic and social condition of districts in Southern England today, which are already reduced to this condition, and reflect upon the vast extension of such a system which might be rendered feasible by the subjection of China to the economic control of similar groups of financiers, investors, and political and business officials, draining the greatest potential reservoir of profit the world has ever known, in order to consume it in Europe. The situation is far too complex, the play of world forces far too incalculable, to render this or any other single interpretation of the future very probable; but the influences which govern the imperialism of Western Europe today are moving in this direction and, unless counteracted or diverted, make toward some such consummation. (*Ibid.*, p. 95.)

The parasites' paradise thus described by Hobson existed indeed, but only in the propagandist dreams of a few ideologists of imperialism, varied by such as Cecil Rhodes, for example, who is quoted as saying:

My cherished idea is a solution of the social problem, *i.e.*, in order to save the forty million inhabitants of the United Kingdom from a bloody civil war, we colonial statesmen must acquire new lands for settling the surplus population, to provide new markets for the goods produced in the factories and mines. The Empire, as I have always said, is a bread and butter question. If you want to avoid civil war, you must become imperialists. (*Ibid.*, p. 72.)

The "colonial statesmen" were, of course, desperately anxious to gain popular support to their empire-building adventures, which would have bankrupted England had not her home industry been expanding considerably faster than the colonial burden. The quotation from Rhodes is only one of the extreme examples of the colonial demagogy. That it had remarkable success is proved by the fact that the tough old revolutionist Engels was "sold" on the idea that the Empire had provided a "feast" in which "the workers gaily share," and however bitter he was about it, he did not deny the "feast." But whether in the dreams of a Rhodes, the propagandist caricatures of a Hobson, or the lamentations of an Engels, the whole idea of a "feast" for England provided by colonial super profits in which even the workers shared was an illusion, behind which was the reality of expanding productivity of the domestic economy with the social wage stimulating its growth—on a small scale the exact counterpart of what was happening to America on a larger scale without even a shadow of empire. And in the third of a century before World War I, although Germany was obsessed with the idea she "needed" colonies, in reality her economic expansion had surpassed the British in rate, precisely because she was not burdened with the parasitism of "empire," and what scraps of empire she had were completely undeveloped.

The spectacle of Engels, one of the most enlightened and educated men of his time, complaining against the whole English working class that it had stupidly fallen under the influence of the bourgeoisie, while in the same sentence he was showing that he was himself a victim of the great hoax of "Empire profits," is a painful one, which should teach humility to all intellectuals who set themselves up as teachers to the working class. For it was the Labour Government in England that finally, when the official claimants to the mantle of Marx were still repeating Engels' mistake as holy writ, discovered and taught the world that the British economy was more prosperous *without* India as a colony than with it. It was far more difficult to discover that "empire does not pay" than to learn that it was morally and politically wrong. The leaders of the French Socialist party still have not learned that lesson.

The illusion of empire was compounded of the most contradictory elements. For the common run of people it was the hope for new Americas, Canadas, and Australias, to which someday they could emigrate and find the fabulous prosperity that eluded them in the homeland. For the "empire statesmen" and adventurers, for the bureaucracy and aspirants to that position, for the *rentiers* and would-be *rentiers,* the illusion was the picture sketched out by Hobson of a homeland devoted to comfortable consumption while production was on the whole shifted over the "backward peoples" who were good for nothing else and would be content with a subsistence —the ancient illusion that low wages meant cheap labor. For the industrialists, on the contrary, the Empire was to consist of consumers of their goods, and certainly not of producers for the world market, which was to remain the monopoly of English industry producing in England. Their classical dream was expressed by the thought that "one yard of cloth per year, added to the back of each one of 400,000,000 Chinese, will keep Manchester textile mills working overtime the year round." All these contradictory illusions jostled one another harmoniously in their common framework of "the Empire," for it is in the nature of a dream world that all contradictions are painlessly resolved—until they are brought into violent collision with the real world.

If even Engels, that stubborn battler against illusions, could be forced to give ground before the grand hoax of a "feast" drawn from exploitation of the colonies, that is indeed witness to the social and political influence it exercised. For it was Engels who, in 1885, destroyed the theoretical foundations for such a concept in his polemic against Eugen Dühring, the book popularly known as *Anti-Dühring*, especially in his three chapters on "The Force Theory." For this illusion, and the dogma that Lenin drew from it of world impoverishment being the basis of enrichment of the industrialized nations, is essentially a return to Dühring's theory of the *political* origin of wealth, as the loot seized from the weak by the strong, the theory of *force* as the decisive element in history. And despite the efforts of the post-Leninist commentators and adapters of the dogma, who have valiantly tried to sustain the dogma in face of the obvious *disintegration of the colonial system* and the equally obvious fact that *America never had a serious colonial system*, the whole illusion of "the profits of Empire" rests upon political subjugation and the monopolies based thereon, of the classical Empire of Great Britain, and when that is taken away the whole illusion evaporates.[2] There is and can be no *eco-*

[2] For example, Paul A. Baran, Professor of Economics at Stanford University, in his *The Political Economy of Growth* (Monthly Review Press, New York, 1957), makes the most sophisticated and professionally competent defense (indirect) of the Leninist thesis on imperialism that has come to my attention. But Baran directs all his marshaling and analysis of evidence to establishing the fact of impoverishment in the underdeveloped countries, and the *intent* of the big powers to profit from it. He *assumes* that the intent was and is successfully carried out, but makes no serious effort to prove it, or to draw the consequences in economic theory. He has quite forgotten the ancient wisdom that there is "many a slip 'twixt cup and lip," that intent is

nomic theory of enrichment drawn from backward lands by the more advanced, without the medium of colonial subjection by political and military force.

The only way in which backward and underdeveloped lands can be made the source of enrichment is through destroying their backwardness, through developing within them the modern means of production—along essentially the same path by which the one-time colonies of the United States, Canada, and Australia developed, where *the most essential step* was the winning of their independence and self-determination. All the "profits" of any other path of development turn out to be illusions, and give way in any over-all balance sheet to a "net loss." And despite the ephemeral weakness of Engels in retreating before the illusion, as in his letter to Kautsky in 1882, the main burden of thought of both Engels and of his leader Marx, *if and when it is freed from the dogmas that were uncritically carried over from the classical political economy,* is a refutation of the whole concept that nations can be enriched by looting other nations. Nations can be enriched only by developing within themselves the modern forces of production; in this process one nation can be helpful to another, but never by subjugating it, which is disastrous for both.

---

not identical with consummation, and that if capitalists were always able to impose their will, "the Revolution" would long ago have disposed of capitalism.

It is slightly amusing to find in some writers, side by side, the most contradictory theories of "imperialist exploitation," as if they supported rather than negated one another. Often we find in one essay or chapter the theory that the colonies are necessary to absorb the surplus product of the metropolis, and thus to postpone the crisis of overproduction, and at the same time that the metropolis grows rich by robbing the colony of its surplus. That is, such theorists are not at all interested in economic analysis, but only in semi-theological exercises in dogma.

IX.

MARX AND LINCOLN

IN THE relations of Marx to Lincoln we find a most accurate index to Marx's relation to America in the broad framework of history.

For Marx it was America and its development that served to mark the emergence of modern society and its main eras. Society emerged from the stagnant Middle Ages when the discovery of America "paved the way" for modern industry and established the world market, in which bourgeois society developed within the shell of the old feudal order of status and authority. In the American War of Independence Marx recognized the dividing line beyond which came the ascendancy of the bourgeoisie, the rise of democracy, and with it modern industry proper. In the American Civil War, Marx saw the opening phase of a totally new era, that of the ascendancy of the working classes. The first of these eras he already registered in the *Communist Manifesto* of 1848; the other two in the Preface to the First Edition of *Capital,* where he wrote:

> As in the 18th century, the American War of Independence sounded the tocsin for the European middle class, so in the 19th century, the American Civil War sounded it for the European working class. (*Capital,* p. 14.)

It was in a letter to Abraham Lincoln, in which he was addressed as "the single-minded son of the working class," that Marx first recognized America as inaugurating the era of the working class. "The workingmen of Europe," he wrote to Lincoln, "feel sure that as the American War of Independence initiated a new era of ascendancy of the middle class, so the American anti-slavery war will do for the working classes." This letter by Marx was written as the Address of the International Workingmen's Association to Abraham Lincoln; it declared on behalf of the European workers "that the star-spangled banner carried the destiny of their class." (*The Civil War in the United States,* Marx and Engels, International Publishers, New York, 1937.)

It is most interesting to note that in the 1840's, when Marx was beginning his economic studies, he was by no means so clear that slavery was so alien to modern society that, if need be, it should be cut out by the sword. Thus, writing to P. V. Annenkov from Brussels, December 28, 1846, in a long criticism of Proudhon, Marx has the following to say:

> Direct slavery is as much the pivot of our industrialism today as machinery, credit, etc. Without slavery no cotton; without cotton no modern industry. Slavery has given their value to the colonies; the colonies have created world trade; world trade is the necessary condition of large-scale machine industry. Before the traffic in Negroes began, the colonies only supplied the Old World with very few products and made no visible change in the face of the earth. Slavery is thus an economic category of the highest importance. Without slavery North America, the most progressive country, would be transformed into a patriarchal land. You have only to wipe North America off the map of nations and you get anarchy, the total decay of trade and modern civilization. But to let slavery disappear is to wipe America off the map of the nations. And therefore, because it is an economic category, we find slavery in every nation since the world began. Modern nations have merely known how to disguise the slavery of their own countries while they openly import it into the New World.

(*Selected Correspondence,* International Publishers, New York, 1942, p. 14.)

Here is a very complex mixture of ideas, which had the most varying influence on Marx's later thought. The idea that open slavery was a *pivot* of modern industrialism disappeared very quickly, and along with it the idea that America without slavery would disappear from the map of nations. The idea of wage labor as only a disguised form of slavery was more persistent, and reappears again and again, but never again in the bald, unmodified form of 1846; and indeed, when we remember that a century later the American trade-union leadership was unanimously to denounce the Taft-Hartley Labor Act as instituting "slave labor" again in America, we will realize it is necessary to be restrained in criticizing Marx for similar thoughts a century ago. Long before the Civil War, Marx was completely clear that slavery was the chief obstacle to modern industrial development. To understand Marx as the passionate warrior against slavery one should study the entire record of his campaign in Europe in support of Lincoln and the North against the Confederacy. And on the narrower aspect of economic theory, Engels was unquestionably expressing his joint opinion with Marx when, for example, he wrote to Weydemeyer, an old associate of the Communist League who became an officer in the Union Army, saying that

> Undoubtedly the outcome of the war will determine the future of all America for centuries to come. As soon as slavery—that great obstacle which fetters the political and social development of the United States—is destroyed, the country will develop with such rapidity that in the shortest time it will secure for itself an entirely different place in world history.[1]

[1] Being unable to find this letter in English publication, I have availed myself of an independent translation from the Russian edition of *Collected Works* of Marx and Engels, Vol. XXXV.

Marx and Engels fully agreed that slavery was incompatible with modern industry, and that sooner or later one would destroy the other. They were not always unanimous as to which side would win the war, however, and their discussion [revealed in *The Civil War in the United States*] provides a most interesting study. I have made a brief selection of quotations to illustrate the point. Marx was from first to last firmly of the opinion that, regardless of the vicissitudes of war, the North *must* win and slavery be extirpated; Engels wavered, and feared the North would lose through sheer ineptitude, weak leadership, and disunity. For example, in a long letter to Marx on July 30, 1862, Engels gave a catalogue of northern failures and weaknesses, which he summed up as follows:

> Furthermore, what cowardice in government and Congress. They are afraid of conscription, of resolute financial steps, of attacks on slavery, of everything that is urgently necessary; they let everything loaf along as it will, and if the semblance of some measure finally gets through Congress, the honorable Lincoln so qualifies it that nothing at all is left of it any longer. This slackness, this collapse like a punctured pig's bladder, under the pressure of defeats that have annihilated one army, the strongest and best, and actually left Washington exposed, this total absence of any elasticity in the whole mass of the people—this proves to me that all is up. . . . In addition, the total lack of talent. One general more stupid than another. No one that would be capable of the least initiative or of independent decision. For three months the initiative once more wholly with the adversary. Then, one financial measure more lunatic than the other. Helplessness and cowardice everywhere, save among the common soldiers. The politicians in like case—just as absurd and devoid of counsel. And the populus is more helpless than if it had lingered three thousand years under the Austrian sceptre. . . . If the North does not proceed forthwith in revolutionary fashion, it will get an ungodly

hiding and deserve it—and it looks like it. (*The Civil War in the United States,* pp. 249–52.)

At first Marx replied to the indictment of the northern leadership by Engels (which by its ironic "honorable" applied to Lincoln, included him also), with a gentle rebuff, saying: "I do not altogether share your views on the American civil war." However, most of his letter (August 7) simply added to the list of northern failures cited by Engels, ending with these words:

> The long and short of the business seems to me to be that a war of this kind must be conducted on revolutionary lines, while the Yankees have so far been trying to conduct it constitutionally. (*Ibid.,* p. 253.)

Engels again wrote Marx on September 9 another scathing indictment of the northern leadership, which closed with these words:

> It is too pitiable, and the lads in the South, who at least know what they want, strike me as heroes in comparison with the flabby management of the North. Or do you still believe that the gentlemen in the North will crush the "rebellion"? (*Ibid.,* p. 254.)

This time Marx answered more forthrightly, and combated the growing defeatism that was clearly taking shape in Engels' mind. On September 30 he wrote:

> As regards the Yankees, I am assuredly still of my previous opinion that the North will finally prevail; certainly the Civil War may go through all sorts of episodes, even armistices, perhaps, and be long drawn out. . . . The manner in which the North wages war is only to be expected from a *bourgeois* republic, where fraud has so long reigned supreme. The South, an oligarchy, is better adapted thereto, particularly as it is an oligarchy where the whole of productive labor falls on the Negroes and the four millions of "white trash" are filibusters by profession. All the

same, I would wager my head that these boys come off second best, despite "Stonewall Jackson." To be sure, it is possible that it will come to a sort of revolution in the North itself first.... It seems to me that you let yourself be swayed a little too much by the military aspect of things. (*Ibid.*, p. 255.)

The revolutionary impatience of Engels, shared in some degree by Marx, was usually confined to their private correspondence, while public writings supported Lincoln's main strategy. Thus it is interesting to note that in his first article on the war written for the New York *Daily Tribune* (September 18, 1861), entitled "The American Question in England," Marx went out of his way to restate that strategy at length, with approval. He wrote:

The war has not been undertaken with a view to put down slavery, and the United States authorities themselves have taken the greatest pains to protest against any such idea. But then, it ought to be remembered that it was not the North, but the South, which undertook this war; the former acting only on the defense. If it be true that the North, after long hesitation, and an exhibition of forbearance unknown in the annals of European history, drew at last the sword, not for crushing slavery, but for saving the Union, the South on its part, inaugurated the war by loudly proclaiming "the peculiar institution" as the only and main end of the rebellion. It confessed to fight for the liberty of enslaving other people.... The Confederate Congress boasted that its new-fangled Constitution ... had recognized for the first time slavery as a good thing in itself, a bulwark of civilization, and a divine institution. If the North professed to fight but for the Union, the South gloried in rebellion for the supremacy of slavery. (*Ibid.*, p. 4.)

But the conflict of opinion between Marx and Engels was, at the same time, a conflict within Marx himself. Again and again the revolutionary rebels against the strategy of constitutionalism. Both Marx and Engels had been thoroughly conditioned by the revolutionary upheavals of 1848, and for them the revolutionary path was the single road to progress; it was in their blood and bones. And in the American Civil War it was the slave power that was revolutionary, while it was the Union that was constitutional and placed the preservation of the *status quo* as the official aim of the war. Their minds told them the Union cause was theirs, but their impulses and instincts made the strategy and tactics of the South more congenial to them. They spoke in their private correspondence of the southern military leaders with open admiration, almost affection, while those of the North are rarely given a good word, and are usually excoriated without restraint. Even Lincoln was included among the "unknown mediocrities," a man with an "aversion to all genius," (*Ibid.*, pp. 98–9) and one from whom only "blunders" were to be expected (*Ibid.*, p. 272).

The one moment when Marx permitted this profound disharmony with the northern leadership to break out in public utterance, with full force, it was indirectly through publicizing the words of another man. Writing in the Vienna *Presse*, to which he contributed thirty-five articles in the course of the war, on August 30, 1862, Marx devotes the whole article to paraphrasing a speech by Wendell Phillips denouncing Lincoln and his "execrable policy." Marx said this speech was "of greater importance than a battle bulletin," and gave it not one word of criticism, even though it crossed the border line of defeatism. The key paragraph, which set the tone for the whole speech, said:

> If the war is continued in this fashion, without a rational aim, then it is a useless squandering of blood and gold. It would be better were the South independent today than to hazard one more human life for a war based on the present execrable policy. (*Ibid.*, p. 203.)

Within two months, however, Marx's reason had overcome his revolutionary prejudices, and we find him writing to Engels to greet the first Emancipation Acts, limited to freeing the slaves belonging to those in arms against the Union. Written on October 29, he still says that he sees "the repulsive side" of the conduct of the war by the North, attributes this to "the nature of 'bourgeois' democracy," but finds the justification for Lincoln's course in its success. He wrote:

> The fury with which the Southerners have received Lincoln's Acts proves their importance. All Lincoln's Acts appear like the mean pettifogging conditions which one lawyer puts to an opposing lawyer. But this does not alter their historic content, and indeed it amuses me when I compare them with the drapery in which the Frenchmen envelops even the most unimportant point. (*Ibid.*, p. 258.)

The "execrable policy" had brought results, within weeks after Marx had approvingly reported Wendell Phillips' denunciation of it as not being worth even "one more human life." And the Marx who respected facts, even when they denied his dogmas or prejudices, was the first to recognize it.[2]

Marx was moving more and more rapidly toward full solidarity with Lincoln. When the elections of 1864 approached, Marx recognized that the threat of revolution in the North was the weapon of the slave power, and not that of the enemies of slavery. He confidently predicted the re-election of Lincoln, and considered it indispensable to world progress.

Even in the earlier years, when Marx and especially Engels displayed their strongest aversion to the northern leadership,

[2] Some three quarters of a century later, the Spanish Civil War showed an analogous inner conflict in the Republican coalition, being assaulted by a combination of "revolutionary" reactionaries assisted from abroad. There the coalition of true conservatives and revolutionists defending the Republic did not reach its goal. The pattern of its inner conflicts can be better understood, however, when viewed in the light of the earlier analogous situation in America.

and even to Lincoln, this had in no way diminished the zeal of their public support of the North. They mobilized labor opinion and action, especially, in that support, and certainly contributed substantially to the defeat of those in England who wanted to intervene on the side of the Confederacy. Their most effective work was conducted through the Central Council (sometimes called the "General Council") of the International Workingmen's Association, of which Marx was a member. There can be no doubt that this support, and its importance, had been noted by Lincoln himself.

When Lincoln had been triumphantly re-elected, the Central Council of the I.W.A. decided that it must adopt an address of congratulations to him. We may suspect that Marx himself had stirred up this idea among the members, notwithstanding his recorded disinclination to participate in such pompous formalities, for he clearly steered the whole matter through the Council, and himself wrote the address. As he reported the matter to Engels, in a letter dated December 2, 1864:

> The worst of such an agitation is that one is much bothered as soon as one participates in it. For example, it was again a matter of an Address, this time to Lincoln, and again I had to compose the stuff (which was much harder than substantial work)—in order that the phraseology to which this sort of scribbling is restricted should at least be distinguished from the democratic, vulgar phraseology. . . .
>
> As the Address to Lincoln was to be handed to Adams [U. S. Ambassador to England], *part* of the Englishmen on the Committee wanted to have the deputation introduced by a member of Parliament since it was customary. This hankering was defeated by the majority of the English and the unanimity of the Continentals, and it was declared, on the contrary, that such old English customs ought to be abolished. On the other hand: M. Le Lubez, like a real *crapaud,* wanted to have the Address made out, not to Lincoln, but to the American people. I have made

him duly ridiculous and explained to the Englishmen that the French democratic etiquette is not worth a farthing more than the monarchical etiquette. (*Ibid.*, p. 273.)

When we read the Address of the Central Council to Lincoln, we realize that Marx took his task with deep seriousness, and by no means as an inconvenient chore with which someone had "bothered" him. What he wrote was the most weighty and clear judgment on the whole Civil War to be produced in that era. Since it is short, we may quote the entire document:

To Abraham Lincoln,
President of the United States of America.
SIR:

We congratulate the American people upon your re-election by a large majority.

If resistance to the Slave Power was the reserved watchword of your first election, the triumphant warcry of your re-election is, Death to Slavery.

From the commencement of the titanic American strife the workingmen of Europe felt instinctively that the star-spangled banner carried the destiny of their class. The contest for the territories which opened the dire epopee, was it not to decide whether the virgin soil of immense tracts should be wedded to the labor of the emigrant, or prostituted by the tramp of the slave driver?

When an oligarchy of 300,000 slaveholders dared to inscribe, for the first time in the history of the world, "slavery" on the banner of armed revolt; when on the very spots where hardly a century ago the idea of one great democratic republic had first sprung up, when the first Declaration of the Rights of Man was issued, and the first impulse given to the European revolution of the eighteenth century; when on those very spots counter-revolution, with systematic thoroughness, gloried in rescinding "the ideas entertained at the time of the formation of the old Constitution," and maintained "slavery to be a beneficent institution, indeed the only solution to the great problem of the relation of labor to capital," and cynically proclaimed property in man "the cornerstone of the new edifice"; then the working classes of Europe understood at once, even before the fanatic partisanship of the upper classes for the Confederate gentry had given it dismal warning, that the slaveholders' rebellion was to sound the tocsin for a general holy crusade against labor, and that for the men of labor, with their hopes for the future, even their past conquests were at stake in that tremendous conflict on the other side of the Atlantic. Everywhere they bore therefore patiently the hardships imposed upon them by the cotton crisis, opposed enthusiastically the pro-slavery intervention, importunities of their "betters," and from most parts of Europe contributed their quota of blood to the good cause.

While the workingmen, the true political power of the North, allowed slavery to defile their own republic; while before the Negro, mastered and sold without his concurrence, they boasted it the highest prerogative of the white-skinned laborer to sell himself and choose his own master; they were unable to attain the true freedom of labor or to support their European brethren in their struggle for emancipation, but this barrier to progress has been swept off by the red sea of civil war.

The workingmen of Europe feel sure that as the American War of Independence initiated a new era of ascendancy for the middle class, so the American anti-slavery war will do for the working classes. They consider it an earnest of the epoch to come, that it fell to the lot of Abraham Lincoln, the single-minded son of the working class, to lead his country through the matchless struggle for the rescue of an enchained race and the reconstruction of the social world.

Signed on behalf of the International Workingmen's Association, the Central Council [by 56 members]. (*Civil War,* pp. 279–81.)

Lincoln answered this Address through the American Ambassador in London, Charles Francis Adams, who addressed A. W. Cramer, the General Secretary of the Central Council of the I.W.A., on January 31, 1865, as follows:

SIR:

I am directed to inform you that the address of the Central Council of your association, which was duly transmitted through this Legation to the President of the United States, has been received by him. So far as the sentiments expressed by it are personal, they are accepted by him with sincere and anxious desire that he may be able to prove himself not unworthy of the confidence which has been recently extended to him by his fellow-citizens, and by so many of the friends of humanity and progress throughout the world. The government of the United States has a clear consciousness that its policy neither is nor could be reactionary, but at the same time it adheres to the course which it adopted at the beginning, of abstaining everywhere from propagandism and unlawful intervention. It strives to do equal and exact justice to all states and to all men, and it relies upon the beneficial results of that effort for support at home and for respect and good-will throughout the world. Nations do not exist for themselves alone, but to promote the welfare and happiness of mankind by benevolent intercourse and example. It is in this relation that the United States regard their cause in the present conflict with slavery-maintaining insurgents as the cause of human nature, and they derive new encouragement from the testimony of the workingmen of Europe that the national attitude is favored with their enlightened approval and earnest sympathies. (*Ibid.*, pp. 282–3.)

Marx wrote to Engels on February 6, to call his attention to the fact that "Lincoln's answer to us is in today's *Times.*" And on the tenth, he wrote again to say:

The fact that Lincoln has replied to us so courteously and to the "Bourgeois Emancipation Society" so rudely and purely formally has made *The Daily News* so angry that it did not print the reply to us. When, however, it saw to its sorrow that the *Times* did so, it had to publish it *belatedly* in the *stop press.* Levy, too, has had to swallow the bitter pill. The difference between L's reply to us and to the bourgeois has made such a stir here that the "Clubs" in the West End are shaking their heads over it. You can understand how much good this does our people. (*Ibid.*, p. 274.)

Less than three months later, Lincoln was dead from an assassin's bullet. Marx wrote to Engels on May 9 that "Today I have to submit an 'Address to President Johnson.'" This document was signed on May 13 by thirty-eight members of the Central Council. We quote those parts dealing with Lincoln:

The demon of the "peculiar institution," for the supremacy of which the South rose in arms, would not allow his worshippers to honorably succumb on the open field. What he had begun in treason, he must needs end in infamy. As Philip II's war for the Inquisition bred a Gerard, thus Jefferson Davis's pro-slavery war a Booth.

It is not our part to call words of sorrow and horror, while the heart of two worlds heaves with emotion. Even the sycophants who, year after year and day by day, stuck to their Sisyphus work of morally assassinating Abraham Lincoln, and the great republic he headed, stand now aghast at this universal outburst of popular feeling, and rival with each other to strew rhetorical flowers on his open grave. They have now at last found out that he was a man, neither to be browbeaten by adversity, nor intoxicated by success, inflexibly pressing on to his great goal, never compromising it by blind haste, slowly maturing his steps, never retracing them, carried away by no surge of popular favor, disheartened by no slackening of the popular pulse; tempering stern acts by the gleams of a kind heart, illuminating scenes dark with passion by the smile of humor, doing his titanic work as humbly and homely as heaven-born rulers do little things with the grandiloquence of pomp and state; in one word, one of the rare men who succeed in becoming great, without ceasing to be good. Such, indeed, was the modesty of this great and good man, that the world only discovered him a hero after he had fallen a martyr. (*Ibid.*, pp. 283–4.)

Our brief retelling of the story of Marx and Lincoln is finished. There was little need for comment, for the story bears its moral for all to see without explanation. Across the gulf of distance that separated Europe from America, and across the greater gulf of social background, education, and conditioning in general, these two so different men found their lives touched, they met in spirit, and meeting they recognized in one another kindred souls enlisted in a common cause and saluted each his comrade.

In Marx's words we have not only a just, precise measurement of the greatness of Lincoln put in the simplest of words; we also at the same time see the greatness of Marx himself who, with his own vision and against his own prejudices and dogmas, could recognize that greatness because he shared it.

It is unfortunate for the world that the followers of Marx have neglected, one might even say they have ignored, the story of Marx and Lincoln.[3] They have completely missed Marx's profound definition of the qualities of the highest leadership. How much nobler and hopeful the world would be today if the words Marx used to describe Lincoln could also have been said of Stalin: "One of the rare men who succeeded in becoming great, without ceasing to be good!" But to Stalin, this side of Marx was "rotten bourgeois liberalism," to be suppressed by the censor and executioner. And the struggle to free themselves of Stalinism remains today the key task of the men and women of a large part of the world. It is a hard struggle, and still to be won. It cannot be won by over-simple clichés about the cult of personality, for it requires a new evaluation of human beings as such. It requires the lessons of the story of Marx and Lincoln.

3 An important exception is the book by Herman Schlüter, *Lincoln, Labor and Slavery,* published in 1913 by the Socialist Literature Company, New York. Despite its great merits, including a compilation of pertinent historical facts, the text of the I. W. A. Addresses, and its valiant attempt to interpret these materials in the spirit of Marx, this work, however, perpetuated the dogmatic position that wage labor is merely a disguised version of chattel slavery, and it ends on the note of an approving quotation from the labor leader, Sylvis, that says: "Even now a slavery exists in our land worse than ever existed under the old slave system." Thus it is an example of how the early Socialist movement in America divorced itself from the mainstream of national working-class development and from the nation's history through dogmatism.

X.

IDEOLOGY AND THE COLD WAR

THE COLD WAR that threatens to be a profound influence on world development for a long time expresses the groping of two super powers, both recent arrivals at the "summit" of power and desperately anxious not to reveal their anxieties, toward defining the necessarily quite new system of world power relationships that must finally emerge. These gropings are expressed simultaneously in tentative power experiments, the period of which seems to be closing, and in ideological struggle, which now is becoming the dominant phase.

A peculiar feature of this struggle lies in the relative absence, compared with previous periods of great power rivalry, of any clearly definable clash of material interests. It would seem that the very intangibility of the issues of division makes the dispute so stubborn and protracted. Certainly both sides are being faced with the stubborn fact that their productive surplus is being more and more consumed in an armaments race that threatens bankruptcy if nothing worse, not to speak of the intellectual and spiritual energies that are squandered with equal prodigality. No possible material gains of a speculative victory for either side could be more than a small fraction of the material sacrifices of the cold war. If the military budgets of the world could be transformed into capital investments in productive equipment, poverty could be abolished in the whole world in one generation.

The governments involved speak different languages for which no translation from one to another has yet been discovered. The debate of ideas, therefore, seems to become ever more sterile, at the official level, but outside the official channels and on the plane of the thinking individual, the struggle of ideologies seems to be entering a new and more productive phase, particularly as it cuts across the line of official orthodoxies on both sides. Our study of *Marx and America,* which deals with an intellectual heritage with roots common to both East and West, may therefore properly be concluded by a look into the origins of the ideological rift between them. It is true that the Marxism-Leninism of the Soviet world has departed far from the original orientation of Marx, and that in the West the thought of Marx, after profoundly changing the whole world of thought, has receded to the background of consciousness. But Marx remains a common ideological link between East and West that, outside the official orthodoxies, will become of incalculable importance.

If Marxism put a deep imprint upon Russia, it must also be said that Russia put an even deeper stamp on Marxism by changing it to what is called Marxism-Leninism. That change in form and direction is important—but on the plane of thought it is a change on the surface. The whole substratum of basic thought remains that of Marx, embodied in millions of printed texts, which furnishes the foundation of intellectual life in the Soviet world. All the regimentation possible cannot wipe out the fact that under the surface of dogma the thought of Marx stems from the western tradition, born in the Mediterranean basin, and flowering in the rise of modern economy and science in Western Europe and America. It must eventually reunite with its source.

The entrance of Marxism into Russian life as a major influence was by way of Lenin and his role in guiding the Russian Revolution. It was the first time in history that Marxism appeared directly in the field of statecraft, shaping governments and their policies. And in 1917 Lenin represented the original thought of Marx, essentially unmodified. How, then, was Marxism given its new line of development by the Russian experience?

Lenin grew up in the school or tendency of the German Social-Democratic party and its ideological leader, Karl Kautsky, one of the original disciples of Marx. Lenin's famous pamphlet, *What Is to Be Done?*, credited with founding the Bolshevik faction of the Russian Social-Democratic Labor party, explicitly recognized Kautsky and the German party as the most authoritative spokesmen of Marxism. Nothing was further from Lenin's mind, when entering the Russian upheaval in 1917, than any idea of revising or reshaping Marx's theory. He had quarreled with Kautsky at the outbreak of World War I about the method of advancing socialism through the war, a quarrel that polarized in two opposing men the two positions that in Marx had been a contradiction in his own thought. Kautsky advocated the utilization of democratic legality, like the constitutionalism of Lincoln; Lenin passionately insisted upon the open revolutionary assault on capitalism at the first big crisis of the war. Each claimed Marx as his authority, and each with reason, though Lenin was appealing to the more spontaneous and dynamic side of Marx. The Marx who penned the Address to Lincoln would have understood and approved of Kautsky. The Marx who wrote that "every social reform remains a utopia until the proletarian revolution" would have claimed Lenin as his own.

When the 1917 upheaval began in Russia, Lenin was in

exile in Switzerland, and out of touch with his party, the war having broken all systematic connections. He immediately matured the idea, brewing in his mind since his break with Kautsky, that the Russian Revolution could be made, given proper leadership, the prelude or trigger that would release the long-maturing German socialist revolution, and propel the cautious Kautskys into action or out of leadership. With Germany plunged into the socialist revolution, Russia could then join the most massive European land to the one most advanced economically, in an unbeatable combination that would carry socialism to all Europe. Lenin never considered the possibility of socialism in Russia alone. Such an idea was never mentioned by a serious Russian leader, until Stalin advanced the slogan "socialism in one country" in 1926, two years after Lenin's death.[1] For Lenin in 1917, the Russian Revolution was to be proclaimed "socialist," not because Russia taken alone was ripe for such a step, but because it would trigger the German socialist revolution.

Marx had himself, together with Engels, adumbrated such an idea a third of a century earlier, and there is little doubt that Lenin was directly inspired by their words in the Preface to the 1882 Russian edition of the *Communist Manifesto,* where they wrote:

> *The Communist Manifesto* had as its object the proclamation of the inevitable impending dissolution of modern bourgeois property. But in Russia we find, face to face with the rapidly flowering capitalist swindle and bourgeois property, just beginning to develop, more than half the land owned in common by the peasants. Now the question is: can the Russian *obschina,*

[1] Stalin recorded his first questioning of the established doctrine in a lecture at the end of 1924, but it was only in 1926 that the issue was placed politically and practically in official debate and went before the entire party and the country.

though greatly undermined, yet a form of the primaeval common ownership of land, pass directly to the higher form of communist common ownership? Or, on the contrary, must it first pass through the same process of dissolution such as constitutes the historical evolution of the West?

The only answer to that possible today is this: If the Russian Revolution becomes the signal for a proletarian revolution in the West, so that both complement each other, the present Russian common ownership of land may serve as the starting point for a communist development. (*Karl Marx: Selected Works,* Vol. 1, p. 192.)

Another example is found where Engels, in an article refuting a Russian writer who thought his country ripe for socialism, made the point, however, that the Russian Revolution would be of the greatest importance for the socialist revolution in the advanced countries "if only because it will destroy at one blow the last, so far intact, reserve of the entire European reaction." (*Karl Marx: Selected Works,* Vol. 2, p. 685.)

Thus, Lenin's theory in 1917 was fully in the spirit of Marx in his most revolutionary moments, and did not challenge any of his theories. The most advanced industrial country of Europe remained the base of strategy, and there was no hint of shifting this base, but, on the contrary, an open declaration that "headquarters" would shift from Moscow to Berlin at the earliest possible moment. Indeed, in a sense, the whole concept may be said to have failed because it was too completely according to Marx, in that it *assumed* the German revolution was ripe, at the exploding point, and only needing a trigger to set it off, and that it did not take America into account, with the new strength and room for growth that America had contributed to European capitalism.

Lenin's strategy was quite new and unfamiliar even to his own party, when he reached Petrograd in April 1917, which may be taken as an indication of how recently it had matured in his own mind. It took him months to win over his own Central Committee, which he himself had formed, and before the seizure of power took place in November, two of its prominent members, Zinoviev and Kamenev, not only voted against it but repudiated it in the public prints. It was almost literally true that the crumbling of the old order had been so sudden and complete that power lay in the gutter waiting for any determined and disciplined group to pick it up; only Lenin was able to crystallize such a group and seize the helm of the Russian Revolution.

How little the Russian Revolution was the result of any plan may be seen by the role of the Soviets, which gave the revolution its name in history. Lenin, whose trigger plan did most to shape the revolution, had noted the rise of the Soviets while he was still in Switzerland, but dismissed them from consideration in anything but a minor role. In arriving in Petrograd, however, he found the Soviets already occupied the position of a "dual power" to the Provisional Government and, even though dominated by opposing parties, more open to quick conversion to his plan than any other public body. The struggle against the Provisional Government made the slogan "All power to the Soviets" a natural tactical development. The slogan was used, withdrawn, and then used again, according to the exigencies of the struggle; but it is significant that in the basic program adopted by the Party Congress, the idea of a Soviet government was excluded, and only a demand for an influential position for the Soviets within the permanent government to be established was put forward. The strategic decision to seize power was independent of the role of the Soviets, and the decision to seize power *in the name of the Soviets,* to proclaim *Soviet power,* was a tactical decision made only on the eve of the act itself. Thus was the actual course of the Revolution, throughout its development, a demonstration that history, however much it may be affected by plans, can absorb them all into a pattern that no one planned because no one could foresee the result of unknown forces.

Lenin's trigger plan might well have succeeded *if the Marxist doctrine of impoverishment had been sound.* If it was an "absolute general law of capitalist accumulation" that the proletariat must become ever more impoverished, there is little doubt that Germany, crushingly defeated in the world war, would really have been ripe for the socialist revolution that Lenin expected, and as Marx had long predicted, and the trigger of Russia would have set off an explosion sufficient to shatter the capitalist order in all Europe. But the German revolution did not come. Capitalist accumulation had not impoverished the masses to make them ready for revolution. Especially in America impoverishment had been avoided, and America gave new strength to European capitalism. All calculations based on the doctrine of impoverishment were unsound and undependable. Lenin could grasp and pull his trigger, but the bomb he expected to explode was not there.

Even the most casual reading of Lenin's speeches and writings during 1917–20 reveals that he was completely depending upon the quick arrival of the German socialist revolution. Again and again he repeated the thought: "If the German revolution does not come, we are doomed." Only when it was clear that the German revolution was indefinitely postponed did he stop speaking of it as "just around the corner." Even then he considered it was postponed for no more than a decade or so. He looked for a means to "hold on" until the German revolution would finally come to the rescue. This means, he thought, was to be found in the New

Economic Policy, which would construct a modified capitalism under the control of a socialist government, based on holding "the controlling heights" of communications, banking, and what was possible in the way of the most modern means of production.

Thus a Marxist Socialist party first took power in the most backward great country, instead of one of the most economically advanced of Europe. It was not a development of the successful application of theory, but it was a dilemma resulting from the breakdown of theory caused by the false dogma of impoverishment.

The situation had not been foreseen by Lenin and the Bolsheviks. They had not chosen it, they had been trapped in it by the utterly unanticipated postponement of the German socialist revolution. And contrary to Lenin's expectation, it was not a postponement for a decade or so, but beyond a second world war and a second German military debacle. No Marxist of any country, Right or Left, would have dared predict in 1917–20 that the German socialist revolution was still at least a half-century in the future! All expectation of help from successful revolutions abroad in advanced industrial countries proved to be the actual utopianism! A socialist political party had taken power under the most unsocialist conditions. To make the dilemma more complete, it was recognized that it was the very backwardness of Russia that had enabled the Bolsheviks to take power, just as it was the advanced state of Germany and of world capitalism that had defeated all attempts to trigger the German socialist revolution.

Lenin became a revisionist of Marxism only under this extreme pressure of history. If he had no modern industrial proletariat, which Marxism held to be the first prerequisite to building socialism, at least he had a socialist governmental power, with which he might hope to create that modern industrial proletariat while waiting for the German revolution. This is the essence of Leninism, as distinguished from the doctrine of Marx. All else that was later incorporated into the "Leninist doctrines" that departed fundamentally from Marxism came after Lenin's death and constituted the first phase of Stalin's regime before he gathered sufficient power to rule directly in his own name. Thus Lenin became the first great dogmatic revisionist of Marx. He took the first step upon what was to become a long, long road that would lead, in the mid-twentieth century, to the point where a socialist ideology openly bases itself upon the backward sections of the world economy and builds them into a block against the countries of the original modern industrial development, on a program of *leaping* from pre-capitalist primitive economy directly into socialism.

To interpret that long road after 1924, however, as the original plan of Lenin and the Bolsheviks, is utter nonsense. Some wiseacres have even repeated an apocryphal quotation ascribed to Lenin, according to which he said that the shortest road to Berlin, Paris, and London was through Peking. Something of the sort was said by Zinoviev, but it was in 1926, long after it was recognized that the road westward had been blocked, and the Russian leadership had been plunged into inner struggle over the way out of the dilemma. But for Lenin the German revolution always remained the *sine qua non* of European and Russian socialism. His revisionism was, in his own mind if not in its historical significance, merely a holding operation. His confident expectation of the German revolution, even if it was delayed, was taken completely from Marx.

Marx and Engels, during most of their lives, expected an early socialist revolution. If the impoverishment doctrine had been valid, it is very probable that their expectations would have been verified in their lifetime. It was only in the years immediately following the defeats of 1848 that they separated themselves briefly from such "revolutionary optimism" and sharply rebuked the romantic revolutionists who always saw revolution just around the corner. This was not only a matter of their temperament, but more profoundly was a necessary conclusion from the impoverishment theory. Thus it may be said that because Marx misjudged the future of America a half-century earlier, Lenin misjudged the immediacy of the German revolution in 1917–20. Events took their course without consulting the dogmas. The dogmas were maintained regardless of events. That is why the relatively small steps of Lenin's revision of Marx were later to lead to the giant steps of Stalinism.

The time and scope of the mass upheaval that was the Russian Revolution were determined by the spontaneous movement of the masses thrown into motion by the disintegration and collapse of the ancient, decayed, anachronistic regime of czarism. Although it had been long expected, when it came there was only one leader who had figured out what should be done with it, where it should be led. That is why it is commonly, but erroneously, believed by opponents and supporters of Lenin alike that he and the Bolsheviks who rallied around him "made the revolution." But the revolution was not made to measure, according to a theory, and when theory was injected into it by Lenin, Russia changed the theory even more than the theory changed Russia.

The attempts to trigger the Western European socialist revolution failed. But they were not without effect. What they released was the counterrevolution, that was to be known as Fascism or Hitlerism, first in Italy and a decade later in Germany itself. The dilemma of the Soviet power grew ever sharper. Where they had looked for help, there grew up the power of a deadly enemy, sworn to exterminate them.

The inner struggles of Soviet leadership all turned on the question of how to break out of the dilemma. Stalin came to power in 1926, though still far from the unconditional power he was to seize in 1934, on the platform of building socialism in Russia from the ground up, with her own resources and regardless of any help from abroad, by means of "forced-march industrialization," the policy known as "socialism in one country." He openly revised the Marxist theory that socialism is the product of high industrialization, and said that for Russia and the underdeveloped nations in general that high industrialization must be the product of a socialist political victory. He repudiated the policy of waiting for the German revolution, and equally the policy of triggering it, which would involve military adventures. The Right oppositions were not homogeneous, but in general wanted to continue the "holding operation" strategy, and even yield more ground internally to capitalist and private economy. The Left oppositions, generally oriented on Trotsky, clung to the trigger strategy and wanted to force the pace of the Western European revolution by military means. Stalin crushed the Trotskyites with the aid of the Right, and then turned on his erstwhile allies and crushed them. After both were defeated they tried, too late, to unite their forces. By 1928 the New Economic Policy was in process of liquidation, "forced-march" industrialization was in full swing under the "Five-Year Plans," and soon the collectivization of agriculture was to follow. The face of Russia swiftly changed. The nation came ever more under a semi-military discipline, like an army on the march, power was ever more centralized—finally into the hands of one man, Stalin.

The rise of the Stalin dictatorship has been given a bewildering variety of explanations. One theory says it is the inevitable unfolding of Marxist theory; another says no, not of Marxist theory but rather of Lenin's revisionism; a third says it was the pattern of "revolution in general," working with "iron inevitability," and that the French Revolution had shown to Russia "the image of her own future" in the rise of Napoleon Bonaparte; a fourth says it was the rise of "mediocrity" or the "mass man" or the "bureaucrat" to rule over men of talent and genius who are the "natural leaders" of a nation; a fifth finds refuge in diabolism, and see the secret of Stalin's rise in his personal ruthless will to power, machiavellian cunning, and criminal lack of scruple, and explains the defeat of his opponents by their lack of similar qualities! And so on. The list of rival theories is a long one. The Stalinists themselves required but one theory, that Stalin was all-wise, all-knowing, all-powerful, and almost, if not quite, divine. The Russian Orthodox Church finally confirmed this theory, and blessed Stalin as God's gift to Russia in her time of troubles. Since the Twentieth Congress of the Communist party, where three years after Stalin's death it was finally recognized that a modern industrial society, to which Russia had grown under the Stalin regime, could not operate efficiently under a medieval political and social order, the Russian leadership has oscillated between diabolism and deification. They have great difficulty finding a golden mean, and are pushed forward and backward, as they face the needs and then the dangers of liberalization.

It should be easier for Westerners than for Russians to get some sort of historical view of Stalin without the aid of any esoteric theories such as those mentioned. Nor need we ascribe the Stalin regime to peculiar traits of the Russian character, although doubtless Stalin did reach back into the past to invoke the sanction of Ivan Grozny and Peter the Great. This was not so much the past determining the present, however, as it was the present dressing itself up in historical costumes to make itself more presentable to society at large.[2]

For Russia in 1926, the choice of alternative leaderships had been narrowed down to the different trends in the Communist party. Possible alternative parties had been driven from public life on the charge, whether just in all respects is

[2] It is interesting to note, for example, that in 1948 Moscow publishers brought out an *English* (as well as Russian and other languages) edition of the *Selected Philosophical Works* of V. G. Belinsky, one of the great figures of the nineteenth-century enlightenment in Russia, a contemporary of Marx, and a molder of the modern Russian mind. I quote a few examples to show how even *liberals* accepted with enthusiasm the concept of the ruthless autocrat (not the benevolent autocrat) as the necessary instrument of progress. Belinsky wrote:

"The Russian people is intelligent and shrewd, zealous and ardent to all that is good and beautiful, when the hand of the father-tsar points out the goal, and when his august voice calls to it." (P. 95.)

"Yes, with us everything had to be started from the top downwards, for at the time when we felt the need of budging from the spot on which we had dozed for centuries, we already found ourselves on a height that others had taken by storm. Of course it was not the people who saw itself at this height . . . but the government, and that in the person of one man—its tsar. Peter had no time to waste: for now it was no longer a matter of securing Russia's future greatness, but of saving her in the present. Peter appeared in good time. . . .

"No, without its Peter, Russia had no possibility of establishing contact with Europe, for she lacked the vital germ of evolution. . . . True, Russia would probably have linked herself with Europe and adopted its civilization without the reforms of Peter, but in the same fashion as India did with England. . . .

"He could not sow and wait calmly until the scattered seed would germinate, sprout and ripen: he cast the seed forth with one hand and wished to reap its fruit at once with the other, in violation of the customary laws of nature and probability—and nature yielded before him her eternal laws, and probability turned into magic. The new Joshua, he stopped the sun midst the sky. . . . He understood that half-measures would not avail and were merely a hindrance: he understood that sweeping changes in things that have been the work of centuries could not be accomplished by halves, that one had to do more than could possibly be done or nothing at all. . . . Be useful to the state, learn,—or die: such was the motto inscribed in blood on the banner of his struggle with barbarism." (Pp. 134–36.)

immaterial, of subservience to foreign powers to buy foreign support. The charge was generally accepted. Given the array of possible choices, in the Russia surrounded by the *cordon sanitaire,* with her experiences in the civil war, with Fascist-like regimes rising all about her, and with the memories of Western military invasions in Europe and the Japanese in Siberia—the victory of the Stalin position, once it was put before the country, was inevitable regardless of the personality of Stalin and what it might mean for the future. Stalin won the country, in the first place, because it had been looking outward too long and too vainly, and Stalin was the first leader who said loudly and clearly that Russia came first. Between Stalin and Trotsky the middle groups were ground to pieces.

This is a "shorthand" picture of a whole era of crisis in a great country, of a complexity defying detailed description. Like all such simplified pictures, it does violence to innumerable details of reality, even if only by leaving them out. But I feel that serious writers of history, regardless of political bias, will eventually interpret Stalin's rise to power as the expression of a nation's overwhelming hunger for her own independent development, and impatience with waiting without end. It was the same force that brought the Chinese Communists to power in China, when Chiang Kai-shek had first destroyed all other alternatives, and then had himself lost the Mandate of Heaven—Chinese version for having made the nation sick of him. It was the same force that was to place Tito and his Yugoslavia in defiance of Moscow, that was to bring Gomulka back to power in Warsaw over the protest of Khrushchev, and to start the major disintegration of the ideology of Stalinism, otherwise known as Marxism-Leninism. The rise of Stalin and the fall of his reputation both spring from the same force, the undying aspiration of nations toward self-determined development.

The detailed differences of program between Trotsky and Stalin were of subsidiary significance, so much so that there were overlapping and interchange between them, according to the momentary exigencies of the power struggle. This has puzzled contemporary historical writers, especially in America, and led them to interpret the inner Russian struggles in very shallow terms. The essential issue being fought out, however, was not even of socialism or variations of socialist thought, but was rather the place of Russia in the world scene.

For Trotsky, Russia, and everything to be done in Russia, was subordinated to the goal of breaking open the road for the Western European socialist revolution. For Stalin, on the contrary, the whole concept of the Western European revolution was a matter for cynical skepticism that later turned into utter indifference. Trotsky was ready to sacrifice Russia to the advancement of socialist revolution in the West. Stalin was ready to sacrifice everything, including the immediate welfare of the Russian people themselves, to make the Russian state which he headed a self-sufficient power, economically and militarily. Trotsky thought as a Western European above nationality, to whom Russia was and must remain, until after the Western European revolution, a semi-barbarian hinterland. Stalin thought as a Russian, convinced, regardless of evidence, that the West was doomed to decline as soon as it lost its monopoly of modern technology. For Trotsky, Russia was a means to an end. For Stalin, the end itself was Russia.

Thus the era of Lenin passed into that of Stalin, and with it died the hope and expectation of someday reuniting the Russian with the Western European socialist revolution. In the era of Stalin, of whom old and stanch Russian monarchists would learn to speak with pride as "Russia's greatest Czar," Russian backwardness was made into a virtue, except in the field of technology, because it sealed off Russia from the pernicious Western influences that Stalin summed up in the contemptuous phrase: "Rotten bourgeois liberalism!"

During the Great Coalition of World War II there seemed to be a new perspective arising so that, when Hitlerism was defeated by the united efforts of East and West, the great ideological schism might be appeased and the conditions for peaceful coexistence of differing systems be realized. That hope quickly disappeared, however, and the cold war took its place.

If a new hope of abatement of the cold war, to some extent at least, is arising now, it represents a certain weakening of orthodox ideologies on both sides, and the rise of a new wave of independent thinking among individuals under the stimulus of the imminent threat of the mutual suicide of atomic war unless something decisive is done to head it off.

Between officials and heads of government it can hardly be expected that this approach to peacemaking will take the form of softening the ideological antagonisms, for the weakening of official ideas among the masses only causes them to be more emphasized and even exaggerated in official circles. Quite regardless of ideology, however, all officials of government feel and must respond to the rising impatience of peoples everywhere against the idiocies of the cold war and especially against the ultimate idiocy of atomic war.

The ideologies are declining in influence, and independent thought is again arising, for many reasons. For one thing, on both sides of the cold war people are asking themselves, how could Russians and Americans carry on sensible and fruitful conversations if the proposed exchange of visitors between the two countries really begins to be carried out? And everyone sees that conversation in terms of the ideological war makes nonsense, and that communication is impossible on such terms. But the difficulty of communication does not arise from the influence of Marx and his thought upon the Russians, but rather from the petrification of that thought into dogmas; while in the West the difficulty does not lie in the rejection of Marx, but rather in the West's implied agreement that the dogmatism of Moscow is really authentic Marxism. Only when all the dogmas on both sides are laid open to question and discussion has the way been opened toward eventual reunification of the world that will make peace something more than an uneasy truce.

We have here merely indicated certain questions about the cold war and its relation to ideology, which are opened up by our study of *Marx and America.* To pursue those questions further would go beyond the scope of this particular study, and must be left to another occasion.

I would close by referring again to the comparison of Marx and Newton in the first chapter, to carry it one step further. Newton's achievements and his greatness so overwhelmed his English contemporaries that after him English mathematical physics was sterile for a hundred years or more, because his disciples could not conceive of doing anything beyond commentary upon his fundamental texts, so that subsequent development in mechanics and mathematics took place on the Continent. There, stimulated by the ambition to compete with Newton, and freed from many of Newton's theological inclinations and the tradition of formal geometric reasoning, new foundations were laid that carried the whole science to new achievements beyond Newton. In the hands of the Russians, after their basic dogmatic revision, Marx suffered the fate of Newton with the English mathematical physicists—he became the object of adoration and commentary, and the very ability to think as Marx thought, extending the frontiers of scientific knowledge, was lost to the Russian Marxists, and they denied the very possibility of improvement on the Marxist method. The renaissance of the fruitful and positive tradition of Marx has begun with the criticisms of Russia's dogmatic distortions of Marx but must proceed to the critical rejection of those dogmas embodied in the original system of Marxism. And even as in the case of Newton, the more we study the errors of Marx, the more do we recognize him as one of the giants in the history of human thought.

INDEX